THE SAFE ROOM

A SANCTUARY FOR GRIEF AND HEALING

Ekene Sabastine Aniakor

Obasi Reloaded Publishing Inc.
Tel: +2348065712051
Email:obasiokoreloaded@gmail.com
Printed in the United States of America.
Cover design by Oko Obasi
ISBN: 9798872778974
Imprint: Independently published
First Edition: December 2023

CONTENTS

The Safe Room

Dedication

This book is dedicated to the memory of Late Mrs. Irene Onyinye Aniakor, my beloved wife, who was seven months pregnant with our twins. She died on May 15th, 2023. May her spirit forever shine bright and may her love continue to guide and inspire those who knew her.

To all grieving people all over the world, this book is also dedicated to you. May its words offer solace, comfort, and hope as you navigate the profound journey of grief. Your strength, resilience, and capacity to love amidst pain are testaments to the human spirit's extraordinary power.

In honoring the memory of Late Mrs. Irene Onyinye Aniakor and acknowledging the experiences of all those who grieve, we strive to create a community of support, understanding, and healing. May this book serve as a beacon of light in the darkest moments, reminding you that you are not alone on this journey.

May the memories of your loved ones remain cherished, and may you find solace, hope, and renewed purpose as you continue to move forward on your healing path.

Acknowledgments

I would like to express my heartfelt gratitude to the following individuals and organizations for their support, guidance, and contributions throughout the creation of this book:

1. Mrs. Ify Nwaneri: Thank you for your unwavering encouragement and insightful feedback. Your wisdom and empathy have been invaluable.

2. Mr. Philippe Marcelis: Your expertise and guidance in grief counseling have shaped the content of this book. Your dedication to helping others on their healing journeys is truly commendable.

3. Chief Charles Egwuoba: Your support and encouragement have been a source of strength. Your belief in the importance of sharing stories of grief and resilience has inspired me.

4. Rev. Sr. MaryAnthony Osakwe Sisters of Jesus the Savior, Ellele Rivers State Nigeria: Thank you for your spiritual guidance and prayers throughout this process. Your faith and compassion have been a guiding light.

5. Chief U.K Charles Egwu: Your unwavering support and belief in this project have been instrumental. Your commitment to fostering healing and resilience is deeply appreciated.

6. Bro. Cyril Uzoma Oghaego Your dedication to providing support and solace to those grieving is truly remarkable. Thank you for sharing your wisdom and experiences.

7. Chief Israel Ajah: Your guidance and support in navigating the

complexities of grief have been invaluable. Your commitment to promoting healing and understanding is commendable.

8. Catholic Education Board, Lafia: Thank you for your support and belief in the importance of addressing grief and healing. Your commitment to community well-being is deeply appreciated.

To the entire staff of Passion of the Wound of our Lord Jesus Christ: Your support, understanding, and patience have been essential in bringing this book to life. Your contributions are deeply valued.

To all the individuals and organizations that have touched my life and contributed to this book in ways beyond those mentioned, thank you. Your presence and support have been vital in shaping this work.

Lastly, I want to express my deepest gratitude to the readers of this book. Your willingness to embark on the journey of healing and to explore the depths of grief is an inspiration. May this book provide solace, comfort, and hope as you navigate your own unique path of healing.

Ekene Sabastine Aniakor
December, 2023

PREFACE

In the quiet corridors of our souls, grief weaves an intricate tapestry, a mosaic of emotions that resonate uniquely with each beating heart. It is a journey both deeply personal and universally shared, drawing us into its labyrinthine embrace. In these moments of profound vulnerability, we yearn for more than understanding; we seek solace, a sanctuary where our grief is not only acknowledged but embraced.

Welcome to "The Safe Room: A Sanctuary for Grief and Healing." Here, within the pages of this transformative book, we extend an invitation to embark on a journey that goes beyond words. It is a journey that promises not just guidance through the tangled paths of grief but a companion—a gentle hand to hold along the way.

In crafting this book, our vision extended beyond mere words on paper. We envisioned a mnemonic, **SAFEROOM**, encapsulating the guiding principles of the sanctuary we sought to create:

- **Support:** Within these pages, find unwavering support as we navigate the intricate landscape of grief together. Offering a hand to hold, a listening ear, and a compassionate heart, we stand as pillars of strength.

- **Acknowledgment:** Your grief is real, and within The Safe Room, it will be acknowledged and validated. We honor the uniqueness of your journey, recognizing the depth of your pain.

- **Fellowship:** Discover a community of kindred spirits who have experienced loss and understand the depths of sorrow. Together, we forge connections, share stories, and provide comfort to one another.

- **Empathy:** The Safe Room is a haven where empathy flows freely. We embrace the power of walking in each other's shoes, offering compassion in the face of pain and understanding the weight of another's grief.

- **Resources:** Practical guidance and resources await you within these pages. From coping strategies to professional assistance, we equip you with tools to navigate the challenges that accompany grief.

- **Openness:** The Safe Room encourages open dialogue and vulnerability. Within this space, you are free to express your thoughts, fears, and emotions without judgment. Authenticity is welcomed and celebrated.

- **Opportunity:** Even in the depths of grief, there are opportunities for growth, healing, and finding meaning. The Safe Room embraces those transformative moments and guides you toward a future filled with hope.

- **Moderation:** Within this sanctuary, we ensure a space that is safe, respectful, and responsive. Our moderation fosters an environment where your voice is heard, and your journey is honored.

Envision The Safe Room—a space that transcends the physical, where walls are built with compassion, and the air is thick with empathy. It is an oasis born from the collective yearning for support, understanding, and practical guidance as we navigate the landscape of loss. Together, we will explore its depths and discover the strength inherent in connecting with others on similar journeys.

Each chapter is a portal, leading you into a different facet of grief. We delve into coping strategies, the significance of seeking professional help, and the delicate art of honoring loved ones while finding meaning in the midst of sorrow. Through real-life stories, practical tips, and a wealth of resources, we weave a tapestry of understanding and support.

In the safety of The Safe Room, open dialogue is encouraged, and vulnerability is met with kindness. Here, shared experiences become threads that weave our stories together, reminding us that we are not alone. Our responsive moderation ensures a space where your voice is heard, your pain is validated, and the hope we collectively nurture becomes a beacon of light.

This book is not a rigid map; it is a compass guiding you through the diverse landscapes of grief. It will help you navigate through triggers, provide guidance for parenting through loss, and offer strategies to cultivate hope even in the darkest moments. The Safe Room stands as your steadfast ally, offering solace and companionship throughout your journey.

As our collective wisdom unfolds, remember that this is not where the journey ends. The Safe Room extends beyond these pages, inviting you to continue your exploration—where healing becomes a shared endeavor, and no heart walks the path alone.

Let this book be the comforting embrace you seek—a source of solace, understanding, and resilience. Within its words, you will find the power to navigate the intricate journey of grief, knowing that you are not alone. Together, within The Safe Room, we will find healing, strength, and the courage to carry on.

As we embark on this journey together, let the mnemonic SAFEROOM guide us, providing a compass to navigate the intricate landscape of grief. Within its embrace, we find support, acknowledgment, fellowship, empathy, resources, openness, opportunity, and the comfort of a safe and moderated space.
We unveil the Sanctuary within The Safe Room!

CHAPTER 1

INTRODUCTION

In the quiet spaces of our hearts, grief often finds its dwelling, weaving an intricate tapestry of emotions that defy easy explanation. It is a journey fraught with complexities, a pilgrimage through the uncharted territories of loss. As we embark on this odyssey together, let us step into the genesis of a sanctuary—the genesis of The Safe Room.

In the annals of my life, there exists a chapter of profound sorrow and loss. I am a widower, having tragically lost my beloved wife, Late Mrs. Irene Onyinye Aniakor, who was seven months pregnant with our twins. The date etched in my memory is May 15th, 2023— a day that forever altered the course of my existence. We had been married for twelve years, from January 4th, 2011, until that fateful day. The journey I embarked upon in the wake of this devastating loss has led me to discover the transformative power of grief and healing—a journey that has been encapsulated in what I now call The Safe Room.

The tragic event of my wife's untimely passing reverberated through my being, leaving me shattered and adrift. The weight of grief settled upon my shoulders as I grappled with the overwhelming emptiness that consumed me. The loss of a life intertwined with mine for over a decade brought forth a torrent of emotions—pain, anguish, and an indescribable sense of longing.

As days turned into weeks and weeks into months, I found solace in the realization that grief is an inherent facet of the human experience. To grieve is Human, to heal is divine! It is through grief that we acknowledge the depth of our love, the magnitude of our loss, and the irrevocable changes that death brings. The Safe Room was born out of the understanding that grief is not a weakness but a testament to the depth of our emotions and our capacity to love.

To lose a cherished partner, especially in such tragic circumstances, is an indescribable pain. The journey of grief is a deeply personal one, yet it is within the realm of shared experiences and empathetic connections that true healing takes root. The Safe Room stands as a testament to the resilience of the human spirit—a sanctuary where grief is acknowledged, support is offered, and healing becomes possible. In my own journey through grief, I have come to embrace the truth that to grieve is human, but to heal is divine. May The Safe Room be a guiding light for all those who seek solace, understanding, and the transformative power of collective healing.

In the Igbo culture, there is a saying, "E buru ozu onye ozo, odika obu osisi ka ebu!" which means that when the corpse of another person is being carried, it appears like a log of wood is what is being carried. This adage highlights the fact that only the person going through the grief truly understands the weight of their sorrow. Life often presents us with traumatic experiences that result in the loss of a loved one—a parent, a spouse, a child, a friend, or someone significant in our lives. This event leaves a profound void, often filled with pain and anguish, triggering a cascade of emotions that can lead to depression.

Tragically, in some cases, it even leads to acts of suicide. It is imperative to provide a safe space for individuals to grieve and heal. Research has shown that there are approximately 132 cases of suicide per day in the United States alone—a staggering statistic that demands attention. Recognizing this, I have dedicated myself to developing strategies to address this crisis. Over the years, I have discovered that individuals who are grieving feel safer opening up to someone who is knowledgeable and not associated with conventional institutions. This realization forms the essence of The Safe Room, a sanctuary designed to provide solace, support, and healing for those in grief.

The Igbo adage, "Eburu ozu onye ozo, odi ka obu osisi kaa ebu," carries a profound message that transcends cultural boundaries. This proverb serves as a poignant reminder to refrain from insensitivity and indifference towards the suffering of others. It emphasizes the importance of empathy, compassion, and acknowledging the shared humanity that binds us all. Within the context of this proverb lies the essence of the safe room, a space that embodies these values and principles.

The safe room is not merely a physical location; it is a metaphorical concept that encompasses an environment of emotional safety, understanding, and support. It is a space where individuals can seek solace, express their vulnerabilities, and find comfort amidst life's challenges. In the safe room, the adage's teachings find practical application.

To truly create a safe room, we must recognize that every person's experiences and struggles are unique. Just as carrying another's corpse feels as burdensome as carrying a log of wood, we must acknowledge that we cannot fully comprehend the weight of someone else's pain or trauma. However, we can choose to meet them with empathy and compassion, treating their emotions and experiences with the respect they deserve.

The Safe Room Initiative is an innovative approach to grief support and counseling that aims to provide assistance to individuals who have experienced profound loss. The founder of the initiative draws inspiration from his own personal tragedies, having lost his unborn twins and his wife during childbirth. He understands the pain, trauma, and grief associated with such profound losses, and he recognized the need for support from others who have experienced similar tragedies.

My own experience highlighted the disconnect I felt when seeking help from individuals who had not gone through a similar loss. This motivated me to create a network of grief survivors who could provide support and understanding to those in need. The Safe Room Initiative seeks to raise an army of grief survivors who can offer support to grieving individuals, families, and communities.

The strategy of the initiative is to replicate the successful approach used in Nigeria, where a group of grief survivors reaches out to help others overcome their own tragedies. The three-pronged approach developed by the founder, based on his personal experience, includes the following principles:

1. It's okay not to be okay: Acknowledging and accepting one's grief and emotions is an important step in the healing process.

2. Escape isolation: Encouraging individuals to connect with others who understand their grief, providing a safe and supportive environment.

3. Keep hope alive: Fostering a sense of hope and resilience, emphasizing that healing is possible even in the face of profound loss.

The Safe Room Initiative has been successful in Nigeria, as grieving individuals feel safe and supported when surrounded by others who have experienced similar losses. The initiative plans to offer both onsite and online programs to cater to those who prefer the anonymity of social media. Additionally, there will be a Safe Room club specifically designed for teenagers and young adults.

By raising a community of individuals who understand and have been trained to provide support, the Safe Room Initiative aims to reduce suicides and offer solace to those who are grieving in the United States and all over the world.

The safe room encourages active listening, genuine understanding, and non-judgmental support. It invites us to leave behind our preconceptions and biases, creating an environment where individuals feel heard, seen, and valued. In this sanctuary of emotional well-being, people can freely express their thoughts, fears, and grief without fear of ridicule or dismissal.

Within the safe room, there is no room for indifference or insensitivity. We recognize that the suffering of others is not a burden to be ignored or dismissed; it is an opportunity for connection and healing. By embracing the adage's teachings, we can foster an atmosphere of unity, where we share the joys and sorrows of our fellow human beings.

Moreover, the safe room encourages us to extend our empathy and compassion beyond our immediate circles. It reminds us that our responsibility to create a safe and inclusive environment extends to society as a whole. We are called to challenge systemic inequalities, discrimination, and marginalization, ensuring that everyone has equitable access to emotional well-being and support.

In the safe room, we acknowledge that healing is not a linear process. Each individual's journey is unique, and we respect the diverse ways in which people navigate their pain, grief, and trauma. We recognize that some wounds may never fully heal, but within the safe room, we provide a refuge where individuals can find solace, understanding, and validation.

The process of healing is a complex and multifaceted one. It is a journey that requires patience, self-compassion, and the support of others who have walked a similar path. The Safe Room became a haven—a sanctuary where individuals like myself, who have experienced profound loss, could find solace, understanding, and guidance. One of the fundamental aspects of The Safe Room is the facilitation of connections between individuals who have endured similar grief. The power of shared experiences cannot be understated. Within this community, empathy flourishes, and the weight of grief becomes more bearable as stories are shared, understanding is found, and a sense of belonging emerges.

The Safe Room community is a refuge, offering a supportive network of individuals who have traversed the arduous path of grief. Here, individuals find validation, compassion, and companionship. In this community, we break the chains of isolation and loneliness, replacing them with connections that provide solace and comfort.

Within The Safe Room, we honor the memories of our loved ones. We celebrate their lives, their legacies, and the profound impact they had on us. Through storytelling, shared rituals, and acts of remembrance, we keep their spirits alive and ensure that their presence continues to guide us on our healing journeys.

The Safe Room: A Conceptual Haven

The Safe Room is more than a virtual space; it is a conceptual haven conceived from the collective yearning for understanding, compassion, and support amidst the tempest of grief. Imagine, if you will, a place where the intangible walls resonate with empathy, where the air is thick with shared experiences, and where the echoes of compassionate hearts create a sanctuary for souls in mourning.

In the pages that follow, we will explore the essence of The Safe Room, understanding its purpose as a guiding light through the tumultuous seas of grief and healing. This chapter serves as an introduction, a key to unlocking the doors of a sanctuary designed to cradle the hearts of those who seek solace.

A Sanctuary's Purpose

The Safe Room is more than a collection of words and ideas; it is a purpose-driven concept crafted to be a sanctuary for individuals navigating the arduous journey of grief. Its purpose is manifold:

1. Acknowledgment: The Safe Room stands as a testament to the acknowledgment of grief—the validation that the pain one feels is genuine, real, and worthy of attention. In this haven, we recognize the significance of every individual's unique journey through loss. The Safe Room is small enough to acknowledge you and large enough to accommodate you!

2. Compassionate Understanding: Within the Safe Room, compassion flows freely. A compassion that embraces and empowers you . It is a place where understanding extends beyond sympathy, embracing the nuances of grief with an open heart. This understanding is the cornerstone upon which the sanctuary is built.

3. Community and Connection: At the heart of The Safe Room lies the vision of fostering a community where individuals connect through shared experiences. This is a place where the isolation often felt in grief dissipates, replaced by a sense of fellowship—a shared journey towards healing. You are never alone.

4. Guidance Through Grief: The Safe Room aims to be a guiding light through the dark alleys of grief. With each chapter, practical insights, real-life stories, and resources unfold to provide not just understanding but tangible tools for navigating the complexities of loss.

5. Hope and Resilience: In the shelter of The Safe Room, the seeds of hope and resilience are sown. It is a place where individuals not only confront their grief but also discover the strength within to emerge resilient and find a renewed sense of purpose.

Embarking on a Journey

As we step into The Safe Room, consider this more than just a conceptual space; think of it as an interactive guide, a companion on your journey through grief. In the chapters that follow, we will explore the pillars that uphold The Safe Room: sympathetic listening, accessible resources, facilitating connections, empowering resilience, responsive moderation, open dialogue, offering validation, meaningful rituals, and so much more.

The Safe Room is a sanctuary, but it is also a dynamic space—an evolving tapestry woven by the stories, experiences, and resilience of those who enter its doors. Together, let us embark on this journey of exploration and healing within the comforting embrace of The Safe Room.

Finding Refuge in The Safe Room

In the profound corners of life where grief resides, we often yearn for a sanctuary—a place where our pain is understood, our journey acknowledged, and our hearts embraced. It is within this yearning that "The Safe Room" comes to life—a conceptual haven designed to cradle those navigating the intricate terrain of grief.

The Safe Room: A Sanctuary for Grieving Hearts

Imagine a space that transcends the limitations of the physical, a place woven with threads of empathy and understanding. The Safe Room is more than a title; it is an invitation into a sanctuary crafted for individuals experiencing grief. Within its virtual walls, we aspire to create an environment where vulnerability is met with compassion, where the silent language of sorrow finds expression, and where healing becomes a collective endeavor.

A Non-Traditional Haven

In the heart of this sanctuary, The Safe Room stands as an unconventional refuge. Departing from the formalities of traditional counseling, it offers an alternative path—a space where individuals can freely explore their grief, unburden their hearts, and connect with others who share the weight of similar experiences.

A Sanctuary Beyond Words

Here, within the virtual walls of The Safe Room, words become vessels for healing. Clients are invited to share their grief experiences openly, knowing that their narratives will be met with empathy and understanding. This space transcends the conventional therapeutic setting, offering a unique avenue for self-expression and communal support.

Guided by Ekene Sabastine Aniakor and Trained Moderators

At the heart of The Safe Room's supportive structure is Ekene Sabastine Aniakor , a compassionate guide who understands the intricacies of grief. Alongside Aniakor, a team of trained moderators is dedicated to facilitating discussions, ensuring that each interaction is not only informative but also nurturing. These moderators create an atmosphere of security, fostering an environment where clients feel heard, valued, and respected.

Seeking Advice, Sharing Experiences, and Meaningful Conversations

Clients within The Safe Room are not passive recipients; they are active participants in their healing journey. Whether seeking advice, sharing personal experiences, or engaging in meaningful conversations, individuals can connect with knowledgeable and empathetic peers who traverse similar paths. The Safe Room becomes a dynamic forum for collective wisdom and understanding.

Supportive and Secure Environment

Ekene Sabastine Aniakor and the trained moderators play a crucial role in upholding the ethos of The Safe Room. Through vigilant oversight, they ensure that discussions remain supportive and respectful, cultivating a secure environment where vulnerability is embraced, and healing is nurtured.

Beyond Tradition, Toward Healing

The Safe Room represents a departure from conventional counseling, offering an alternative that recognizes the diversity of grief experiences. It invites individuals to step into a space where empathy reigns supreme, conversations are meaningful, and healing transcends the boundaries of tradition. As we embark on this journey within The Safe Room, let it be a testament to the transformative power of collective support and understanding. Together, we will forge a path beyond tradition, toward healing and resilience.

This book unfolds with a clear purpose—to guide and support you through the labyrinth of grief and onto the path of healing. We embark on a journey together, recognizing the uniqueness of each grief-stricken heart and the universality of the emotions that bind us.

Guiding You through the Journey of Grief and Healing

The aim of this book is simple yet profound: to be a companion through your grief journey. We acknowledge the complexity of grief, the myriad emotions it evokes, and the challenges it poses. The Safe Room is not just a theoretical concept; it's a guiding philosophy that informs each chapter, offering practical insights, empathetic narratives, and resources to light your way.

What to Expect

In the chapters that follow, we will delve into the pillars that uphold The Safe Room. From the importance of sympathetic listening to the power of meaningful rituals, each section is tailored to provide guidance, understanding, and a sense of community. Through shared stories, practical tips, and a wealth of resources, we aspire to be more than words on paper—we aim to be a source of solace and strength.

You Are Not Alone

As you turn the pages, remember that you are not alone in your journey. The Safe Room is not just a destination; it's a shared space where grief is met with empathy, where stories intertwine, and where healing becomes a communal effort.

Closing Thoughts

In the sanctuary of The Safe Room, we invite you to embrace your grief, to explore its contours, and to find the strength within to navigate this transformative journey. The purpose of this book is not just to guide you through grief but to illuminate the path to healing, offering you a haven—a Safe Room—for your heart to find solace and renewal. Welcome to a space where your journey is seen, acknowledged, and embraced.

CHAPTER 2

SYMPATHETIC LISTENING

The Art of Compassionate Understanding

In the intricate dance of grief, where emotions ebb and flow like tides, the profound impact of empathetic and compassionate listening cannot be overstated. Chapter 2 of "The Safe Room" is an exploration of the transformative power of Sympathetic Listening— a fundamental pillar within our sanctuary that fosters understanding, connection, and healing.

Understanding the Importance of Empathetic Listening

Grief is a language often spoken in silence, in the nuances between words, and in the unspoken depths of the heart. Within The Safe Room, the essence of Sympathetic Listening lies in the acknowledgment that everyone's grief journey is unique. By offering empathetic and compassionate listening, we recognize the significance of each individual's experience and create a space where their pain is seen and understood.

The Healing Power of Presence

In a world saturated with noise, the simple act of being present and attuned to someone's grief can be profoundly healing. Sympathetic Listening is not just about hearing words; it's about understanding the emotions embedded within them. Within The Safe Room, we strive to create an environment where clients feel heard, validated, and supported—a sanctuary where the healing power of presence is embraced.

Grief is a deeply personal and complex journey that individuals navigate in their own unique ways. In times of grief, the art of compassionate understanding becomes especially crucial. It provides a compassionate framework for supporting those who are grieving and fosters healing, connection, and empathy. In this chapter, we will explore how the art of compassionate understanding can be applied specifically to the context of grief, offering insights and strategies for supporting others and navigating our own grief journeys with compassion.

Cultivating Compassionate Understanding in Grief

Honoring Individual Experiences

Grief is a deeply personal experience, and each person's journey is unique. Compassionate understanding acknowledges and respects the individual's unique process, allowing space for their emotions, thoughts, and coping mechanisms to unfold without judgment or comparison.

Active Presence and Listening

When supporting someone in grief, the art of compassionate understanding involves being actively present and providing a safe space for them to express their feelings. Active listening, without interruption or judgment, demonstrates empathy and creates a supportive environment for them to share their thoughts and emotions.

Validating Emotions

Compassionate understanding acknowledges and validates the wide range of emotions experienced in grief, including sadness, anger, guilt, or confusion. It involves expressing empathy and validating these emotions, allowing the grieving person to feel heard and understood without trying to fix or diminish their feelings.

Practical Strategies for Compassionate Understanding in Grief

Practicing Empathy and Perspective-Taking

Empathy plays a pivotal role in compassionate understanding during grief. By actively putting ourselves in the shoes of the grieving person, we can gain insight into their experience and respond with greater understanding and compassion.

Avoiding Assumptions and Providing Space for Expression

In times of grief, it is crucial to avoid making assumptions about what the grieving person needs or feels. Instead, create a safe and non-judgmental space for them to express themselves authentically. Allow them to guide the conversation and share their memories, thoughts, and emotions at their own pace.

Offering Practical Support

Compassionate understanding extends beyond emotional support. Practical acts of kindness, such as preparing meals, running errands, or offering assistance with funeral arrangements, can alleviate some of the burdens that grieving individuals may face. These gestures demonstrate compassion and help create a supportive environment.

Educating Yourself about Grief

To deepen your compassionate understanding, take the initiative to educate yourself about grief and its various aspects. Read books, attend workshops, or seek guidance from grief counselors. This knowledge equips you with valuable insights and helps you provide more informed and empathetic support.

Creating a Safe Haven for Expression

Within The Safe Room, Sympathetic Listening is not just a skill— it's a commitment to creating a safe haven for expression. By embracing the art of compassionate understanding, participants can traverse the landscapes of grief with the reassurance that their voices will be heard and their stories valued.

Practical Tips for Sympathetic Listening within The Safe Room

1. Cultivating Presence:

- Encourage participants to be fully present during discussions.

- Discourage distractions, emphasizing the importance of focused attention.

2. Non-Verbal Cues:

- Guide individuals in using non-verbal cues such as nodding, eye contact, and gentle gestures to convey understanding.

- Train moderators to be attuned to these cues, ensuring they respond appropriately.

3. Validation Techniques:

- Teach the art of validation—acknowledging and affirming the emotions expressed without judgment.

- Share phrases that convey empathy, such as "I hear you," or "Your feelings are valid."

4. Reflective Listening:

- Advocate for reflective listening, encouraging participants to paraphrase or reflect back what they've heard to ensure mutual understanding.

- Train moderators to use reflective techniques to enhance the quality of discussions.

5. Open-Ended Questions:

- Guide participants in asking open-ended questions that invite deeper sharing.

- Encourage moderators to employ open-ended queries to prompt meaningful conversations.

6. Patience and Silence:

- Emphasize the value of patience, allowing individuals to express themselves at their own pace.

- Train moderators to appreciate the potency of silence, recognizing that sometimes, words alone cannot capture the depth of grief.

As we delve into the intricacies of Sympathetic Listening within The Safe Room, let this chapter be an invitation to cultivate a deeper connection—one conversation at a time, one heart at a time. Together, let us explore the profound healing that unfolds when ears listen not just to words but to the unspoken echoes of grief.

Conclusion:

The art of compassionate understanding is a guiding light in times of grief. By honoring individual experiences, practicing active presence and listening, and validating emotions, we create a nurturing environment for healing and support. Through empathy, perspective-taking, avoiding assumptions, offering practical assistance, and educating ourselves about grief, we deepen our capacity to provide compassionate understanding to those who are grieving. Let us embrace this art and walk alongside others with empathy, love, and understanding as they navigate their grief journeys.

CHAPTER 3

ACCESSIBLE RESOURCES

In the journey of grief, knowledge can be a beacon of light, guiding individuals through the intricate paths of healing. Chapter 3 of "The Safe Room" is a testament to the profound significance of Accessible Resources—a commitment to ensuring that support and information are readily available to empower and comfort those navigating the complex terrain of grief.

Nurturing grief support through knowledge is a valuable approach to providing compassionate and informed assistance to those who are grieving. Here are some ways to cultivate knowledge and enhance grief support:

1. Educate Yourself: Take the initiative to educate yourself about grief and the grieving process. Read books, articles, or reliable online resources on grief, loss, and bereavement. Attend workshops or seminars on grief counseling or support. By gaining knowledge about grief, you can better understand its complexities and offer informed support.

2. Understand Different Grief Experiences: Recognize that grief is a highly individual and diverse experience. Learn about the various ways people grieve, including cultural and religious differences in grieving practices. Understanding these differences will help you approach each person's grief journey with sensitivity and respect.

3. Learn about Common Reactions to Grief: Familiarize yourself with the common emotional, physical, and cognitive reactions that individuals may experience while grieving. This includes understanding common symptoms such as sadness, anger, guilt, changes in appetite or sleep patterns, difficulty concentrating, or feelings of numbness. Knowing these reactions can help you normalize their experiences and offer appropriate support.

4. Be Aware of Complicated Grief: Educate yourself about complicated grief, which refers to an intense, prolonged, or debilitating form of grief that may require professional intervention.

Understand the signs and symptoms of complicated grief, such as persistent feelings of intense longing, difficulty accepting the loss, or an inability to engage in daily activities. This knowledge can help you identify when someone may need additional support from a grief counselor or therapist.

5. Recognize Supportive Resources: Familiarize yourself with local grief support resources, such as bereavement support groups, counseling services, or helplines. Be aware of organizations or online communities that specialize in grief support. Having this knowledge allows you to provide referrals and connect grieving individuals with appropriate resources for ongoing support.

6. Practice Active Listening and Empathy: Apply your knowledge by actively listening to the grieving person's experiences and emotions. Show empathy and validate their feelings. Avoid offering unsolicited advice or trying to "fix" their grief. Instead, create a safe space for them to express themselves and provide compassionate support based on your understanding of grief.

7. Be Mindful of Self-Care: While supporting others in grief, it is essential to prioritize your own self-care. Educate yourself on self-care strategies and coping techniques for grief supporters. This knowledge will help you maintain your own well-being, ensuring that you can provide sustained support to others.

The Significance of Accessible Resources in Grief Support
Grief, in its myriad forms, can be a labyrinth of confusion and

uncertainty. Providing easily accessible resources serves as a lifeline, offering clarity, guidance, and a sense of empowerment to individuals experiencing loss. This chapter explores the pivotal role that readily available information plays in fostering resilience and aiding the healing process within The Safe Room.

Empowering Through Knowledge

Within The Safe Room, we recognize that knowledge is a powerful tool in the hands of those traversing grief. Accessible Resources are not merely informational; they are empowering tools that equip individuals with the insights, strategies, and perspectives needed to navigate the multifaceted journey of healing.

A Diverse Range of Resources within the Safe Room Platform

1. Educational Articles and Guides:

- Curate a library of articles and guides addressing various aspects of grief, from understanding the stages of mourning to coping strategies for different types of loss.

- Ensure that these resources are written in an accessible and empathetic tone, providing both information and comfort.

2. Interactive Workshops and Webinars:

- Host live and recorded workshops facilitated by grief experts, covering topics such as coping mechanisms, self-care practices, and fostering resilience.

- Enable participants to engage in Q&A sessions, promoting a sense of community and shared learning.

3. Personal Stories and Testimonials:

- Feature a collection of personal narratives from individuals who have navigated their grief journey successfully.

- Highlight the diversity of experiences to validate the uniqueness of each individual's path.

4. Creative Outlets and Expressive Arts:

- Introduce resources that leverage creative expressions such as art, writing, and music to provide therapeutic outlets for grief.

- Collaborate with artists and therapists to create interactive activities within The Safe Room.

5. Resource Directory:

- Develop a comprehensive directory of external resources, including helplines, support groups, and mental health professionals specializing in grief counseling.

- Ensure that this directory is regularly updated and easily accessible within The Safe Room platform.

6. FAQs and Quick Reference Guides:

- Compile a set of frequently asked questions and concise reference guides addressing common concerns related to grief.

- Make these resources readily available for quick access during moments of uncertainty.

Navigating Grief with Informed Compassion

Access to a diverse range of resources within The Safe Room is not just about information; it's about extending a compassionate hand equipped with knowledge. Whether seeking practical advice, emotional support, or creative outlets for expression, individuals within The Safe Room are encouraged to explore a wealth of resources tailored to meet their unique needs.

This chapter serves as an affirmation of our commitment to nurturing an informed, supportive, and accessible environment within The Safe Room. By empowering individuals with knowledge, we strive to illuminate the path to healing and remind those in grief that they are not alone on their journey.

The Significance of Easily Accessible Resources

In the realm of grief support, providing easily accessible resources is of paramount importance. Grief can be a complex and overwhelming experience, and individuals navigating this journey require readily available information, guidance, and support. By ensuring accessibility, The Safe Room acknowledges the diverse needs of its community and empowers individuals to find the resources that resonate with their unique circumstances.

Empowering Through Information and Support

1. Education and Understanding: Accessible resources offer educational materials that help individuals understand the various dimensions of grief. They provide insights into the emotional, physical, and psychological aspects of loss, empowering individuals with knowledge to navigate their grief journey.

2. Coping Strategies and Tools: Resources within The Safe Room equip individuals with practical coping strategies and tools to manage their grief. These may include relaxation techniques, mindfulness exercises, journaling prompts, and self-care practices that promote healing and resilience.

3. Professional Guidance: Accessible resources connect individuals to professional grief counselors, therapists, and support groups. They provide information on how to access these services, ensuring that individuals have avenues for seeking specialized help when needed.

4. Peer Support: Resources that facilitate peer support create opportunities for individuals to connect with others who have experienced similar losses. These platforms, whether online forums, discussion boards, or virtual support groups, foster a sense of belonging and reduce the isolation often associated with grief.

5. Creative Outlets: Accessible resources may include creative outlets such as art therapy exercises, writing prompts, or music playlists that allow individuals to express their grief in non-verbal and cathartic ways. These outlets can be particularly beneficial for those who struggle with verbalizing their emotions.

The Diverse Range of Resources within The Safe Room Platform

1. Articles and Blog Posts: The Safe Room offers a rich collection of

articles and blog posts written by grief experts, psychologists, and individuals who have navigated their own grief journeys. These resources cover a wide range of topics, including coping strategies, self-reflection exercises, and personal stories of healing.

2. Guided Meditations and Mindfulness Practices: The Safe Room provides a library of guided meditations and mindfulness practices tailored to grief and healing. These resources offer individuals a chance to cultivate inner peace, reduce anxiety, and develop a deeper connection with themselves and their grief.

3. Recommended Reading List: The Safe Room curates a list of recommended books, both fiction and non-fiction that explore themes of grief, loss, and resilience. This literary collection offers solace, inspiration, and different perspectives on the grieving process.

4. Resource Directories: The Safe Room houses comprehensive directories that connect individuals to professional grief counselors, therapists, and support groups. These directories provide information on practitioners specializing in grief support, ensuring that individuals can access the professional help they may need.

5. Interactive Workbooks and Worksheets: The Safe Room offers interactive workbooks and worksheets that guide individuals through self-reflection exercises, journaling prompts, and activities designed to promote healing and self-discovery. These resources encourage individuals to engage actively in their grief journey.

6. Virtual Support Groups and Discussion Forums: The Safe Room provides virtual support groups and discussion forums where individuals can connect with others who share similar experiences. These platforms foster a sense of community, allowing individuals to share their stories, seek advice, and offer support to one another.

By offering a diverse range of easily accessible resources within The Safe Room, individuals in grief can find the information, support, and tools they need to navigate their unique journeys. These resources empower individuals, promote healing, and reinforce the sense of community within The Safe Room platform.

Remember that knowledge alone is not enough; it is the application of that knowledge through compassionate actions that truly nurtures grief support. By combining your understanding of grief with empathy, active listening, and ongoing learning, you can offer meaningful and informed support to those who are grieving.

CHAPTER 4

FACILITATING CONNECTIONS

In the intricate tapestry of grief, the threads of connection can be powerful anchors, weaving together hearts that share a common language of loss. Chapter 4 of "The Safe Room" unravels the significance of Facilitating Connections—a purposeful effort to bring individuals who have experienced similar grief together within our virtual sanctuary.

The Role of Facilitating Connections in Grief Support

Grief, though deeply personal, can be isolating. Facilitating Connections within The Safe Room is not merely about creating a virtual gathering space; it's about forging pathways for individuals to reach out and find solace in the shared understanding of those who have walked similar paths. This chapter explores the role of connection in the healing process and the intentional efforts made within The Safe Room community.

Building a Supportive Network

1. Shared Experiences:

    - Encourage participants to share their grief narratives, fostering a sense of vulnerability and openness.

    - Highlight the commonalities in experiences to help individuals recognize that they are not alone in their feelings and struggles.

2. Structured Support Groups:

    - Organize support groups based on specific types of loss or common themes, creating smaller, more intimate communities within

The Safe Room.

- Facilitate regular group discussions, providing a platform for participants to share, empathize, and learn from one another.

3. Peer Mentorship Programs:
- Establish mentorship programs where individuals who have progressed further in their grief journey can offer guidance and support to those who are newer to the process.
- Encourage the exchange of insights, coping strategies, and personal growth stories.

4. Interactive Forums and Discussions:
- Create dedicated forums for open discussions on various aspects of grief.
- Foster an environment where participants can ask questions, offer advice, and engage in meaningful conversations, building a sense of camaraderie.
Facilitating connections is a powerful way to provide support and comfort to individuals who are grieving. By fostering connections, you can create a sense of community, empathy, and understanding. Here are some ways to facilitate connections in the context of grief:

1. Support Groups: Encourage the grieving person to join a grief support group. These groups provide a safe space for individuals to connect with others who have experienced similar losses. Group members can share their stories, offer support, and provide a sense of belonging. Research local support groups or online communities that cater to various types of loss.

2. Introduce Shared Experiences: If you know someone who has

gone through a similar loss, consider connecting them with the grieving person. This can be done through introductions, facilitated conversations, or simply sharing stories of others who have navigated similar grief journeys. Connecting with someone who has walked a similar path can provide validation, empathy, and the realization that they are not alone.

3. Arrange Social Gatherings: Organize informal gatherings or events where friends, family, or supportive individuals can come together to remember the person who has passed away. These gatherings can be casual, such as a potluck dinner, a memorial walk, or a virtual gathering, allowing people to share stories, memories, and emotions in a supportive environment.

4. Encourage Open Communication: Create an atmosphere where open and honest conversations about grief are welcome. Encourage the grieving person to express their feelings and thoughts to friends, family, or a trusted support network. By fostering open communication, you help break down barriers and create opportunities for genuine connections.

5. Share Resources: Provide resources, such as books, articles, or podcasts, that address grief and healing. Recommending these resources can help the grieving person feel supported, validated, and connected to a broader community of people who have experienced similar losses.

6. Volunteer or Donate: Encourage the grieving person to channel

their grief into meaningful actions by volunteering or donating to organizations related to their loved one's cause or interest. Engaging in activities that honor the memory of the person who passed away can create a sense of purpose and connection with others who share similar passions.

7. Offer Continued Support: Grief is not a linear process, and connections need to be nurtured over time. Check in regularly with the grieving person to see how they are doing and offer ongoing support. Continue to facilitate connections by being present, listening, and showing empathy as they navigate their grief journey.

The Role of Facilitating Connections

Within The Safe Room, one of the core objectives is to facilitate connections between individuals who have experienced similar grief. These connections play a vital role in offering support, empathy, and a sense of belonging. By fostering a community where individuals can connect, share, and learn from one another, The Safe Room creates a space for collective healing and resilience.

The Benefits of Finding Support and Building Connections

1. Validation and Understanding: Connecting with others who have experienced similar grief provides a profound sense of validation. When individuals share their stories and find understanding in others' experiences, they realize that they are not alone in their pain. This validation fosters a sense of normalcy and helps individuals navigate the complexities of their grief.

2. Empathy and Compassion: Building connections within The Safe Room community cultivates a foundation of empathy and compassion. Individuals who have walked similar paths can offer genuine understanding, support, and comfort to one another. This exchange of empathy creates a safe and nurturing environment where individuals feel seen, heard, and valued.

3. Shared Wisdom and Coping Strategies: Within The Safe Room, individuals can share their personal insights, coping strategies, and lessons learned from their grief journeys. This collective wisdom empowers others to explore new approaches, discover coping mechanisms, and find inspiration in the resilience of their peers.

4. Reduced Isolation and Loneliness: Grief can often lead to feelings of isolation and loneliness. By building connections within The Safe Room, individuals find a community where they can connect with others who truly understand their experiences. This connection combats the isolation and provides a supportive network of individuals who offer companionship and solace.

5. Emotional Support and Companionship: The Safe Room community becomes a source of emotional support and companionship. Individuals can engage in conversations, share their challenges, and receive encouragement from others who have faced similar circumstances. This support system helps alleviate the emotional burden of grief and provides comfort during difficult times.

6. Inspiration and Hope: Witnessing the healing journeys of others within The Safe Room community can inspire hope. When individuals see others moving forward and finding meaning in the midst of their grief, it offers a glimmer of possibility and resilience. This shared hope becomes a catalyst for personal growth and transformation.

7. Breaking Stigma and Normalizing Grief: By connecting with others who have experienced grief, individuals contribute to breaking the stigma surrounding grief. They help normalize the grieving process and create a space where open conversations about loss and healing are welcomed. This normalization fosters greater understanding and support within society as a whole.

The Safe Room Community: A Haven for Connection

The Safe Room provides a haven where individuals can build connections and find support within a compassionate community. By facilitating these connections, The Safe Room embraces the power of shared experiences, empathy, and collective healing. It becomes a place where individuals can find solace, strength, and a renewed sense of hope as they navigate their grief journeys together.

As individuals connect within The Safe Room community, they contribute to their own healing while also offering support to others. The power of these connections lies in the shared wisdom, understanding, and empathy that create an environment of profound healing and resilience.

Facilitating Connections

Facilitating connections within The Safe Room community involves creating opportunities for individuals to connect with others who have experienced similar types of grief or losses. This can be done through various means, such as virtual support groups, discussion forums, or even personalized matching based on shared experiences. The goal is to foster a sense of belonging and create a space where individuals can find comfort, understanding, and support from others who can relate to their unique journeys.

Within The Safe Room, facilitating connections often involves:

1. Group Settings: Virtual support groups or discussion forums are structured environments where individuals can come together to share their stories, exchange insights, and support one another. These groups are often led by trained facilitators who create a safe and inclusive space for open dialogue.

2. Personalized Matching: The Safe Room may offer personalized matching based on shared experiences or specific types of losses. This allows individuals to connect with others who have gone through similar circumstances, facilitating deeper understanding and empathy.

3. Community Events: The Safe Room may organize community events, such as webinars, workshops, or virtual gatherings, where individuals can come together to learn, share, and connect. These

events provide opportunities for individuals to build relationships, share their experiences, and find support.

Benefits of Finding Support and Building Connections

Finding support and building connections within The Safe Room community offers numerous benefits for individuals navigating their grief journeys. Some of these benefits include:

1. Emotional Validation: Connecting with others who have experienced similar grief validates one's emotions and experiences. It helps individuals realize that their feelings are normal and understandable, reducing any self-doubt or isolation they may feel.

2. Peer Learning and Wisdom: Within The Safe Room community, individuals can learn from the experiences and insights of others. They can gain new perspectives, discover coping strategies, and find inspiration in the resilience of their peers.

3. Increased Coping Skills: Building connections allows individuals to learn effective coping skills from others who have faced similar challenges. They can gain practical advice, try out different techniques, and discover what works best for them in their grief journey.

4. Supportive Network: The connections formed within The Safe Room provide a supportive network of individuals who understand and empathize with each other's pain. This network offers companionship, encouragement, and a listening ear during difficult

times.

5. Reduced Feelings of Isolation: Grief often brings a sense of isolation and loneliness. By connecting with others who have experienced similar losses, individuals can break free from this isolation and find a community where they feel understood and supported.

6. Shared Hope and Inspiration: Witnessing the healing journeys of others within The Safe Room community can inspire hope and provide a source of motivation. Seeing others find meaning and growth in their grief can instill a sense of possibility and resilience in one's own journey.

7. Breaking Stigma and Building Awareness: By connecting with others and sharing their experiences, individuals contribute to breaking the stigma surrounding grief. They help raise awareness and understanding about the complexities of grief, fostering greater support and empathy within society.

Overall, finding support and building connections within The Safe Room community offers a range of benefits, from emotional validation and learning to reduced isolation and increased resilience. It creates a space where individuals can find solace, strength, and a renewed sense of hope as they navigate their grief journeys together.

Benefits of Building Connections in the Safe Room Community
1. Validation and Understanding:

- Connecting with others who have experienced similar grief validates individual experiences, fostering a profound sense of understanding.

- Participants can find solace in knowing that their emotions are acknowledged and shared by others within The Safe Room community.

2. Reducing Isolation:

- Facilitating connections diminishes the sense of isolation often experienced in grief.

- The Safe Room becomes a space where individuals realize they are part of a collective journey, and the burden of grief is shared.

3. Strengthening Resilience:

- Through shared stories of resilience and growth, individuals are inspired to navigate their grief journey with newfound strength.

- Witnessing others who have faced similar challenges and emerged resilient instills hope and encouragement.

4. Creating a Supportive Ecosystem:

- The connections formed within The Safe Room extend beyond the virtual realm, creating a supportive ecosystem that transcends time and space.

- Participants find not just peers but companions who walk with them on their unique paths of healing.

In The Safe Room, You Are Not Alone

The intentional act of facilitating connections within The Safe Room is an affirmation—a declaration that, in grief, individuals are not alone. As participants reach out and intertwine their threads of experience, they contribute to a community where understanding flourishes, resilience thrives, and the healing journey becomes a shared endeavor. Chapter 4 invites individuals to not only find comfort in their shared grief but to also discover the strength that arises when hearts connect in the pursuit of healing.

Remember that facilitating connections requires sensitivity and respect for each person's unique needs and preferences. Not everyone may be ready or comfortable with certain forms of connection, so it's important to be mindful and understanding of their boundaries. By creating opportunities for connection, you can help individuals find solace, support, and a sense of community in the midst of their grief.

CHAPTER 5

EMPOWERING RESILIENCE

In the depths of grief, it can often feel as though the pain will never subside, and the weight of loss will forever bear down upon us.

However, within The Safe Room, we recognize the immense potential for resilience that lies dormant within each individual. It is through the empowerment of resilience that healing becomes possible. In this chapter, we will explore the importance of fostering resilience in the face of grief and outline strategies and exercises offered within The Safe Room to facilitate this empowering process.

The Importance of Resilience in Grief

Acknowledging the Transformative Power of Resilience

Resilience is not the absence of pain or the erasure of grief. Rather, it is the ability to navigate and adapt to the challenges that arise from loss. By acknowledging the transformative power of resilience, individuals within The Safe Room community understand that they possess the inner strength necessary to move forward in their healing journeys.

Building Emotional Strength

Grief can leave us emotionally vulnerable, making it essential to cultivate emotional strength. Resilience empowers individuals to acknowledge and process their emotions, providing a solid foundation for healing and growth.

Moving from Surviving to Thriving

Resilience allows individuals to move beyond mere survival and embrace a life of purpose, joy, and meaning. It provides the framework for transforming pain into personal strength and finding new paths to happiness.

Strategies for Building Resilience

Cultivating Self-Compassion

Within The Safe Room, self-compassion is recognized as a vital component of resilience. Individuals are guided to treat themselves with kindness, understanding, and forgiveness. Through self-compassion practices, such as self-care routines, mindfulness exercises, and positive affirmations, they learn to navigate grief with gentleness and love.

Seeking Support and Connection

Isolation can hinder resilience, making it crucial to foster connections within The Safe Room community. Through virtual support groups, discussion forums, and personalized matching, individuals find solace in the shared experiences and understanding of others. Building connections provides a network of support that bolsters resilience and reminds individuals they are not alone on their journey.

Developing Coping Strategies

The Safe Room offers a range of coping strategies tailored to individual needs. From journaling and creative expression to meditation and breathing exercises, these techniques provide tools for navigating grief and building resilience. Participants are encouraged to explore and experiment with different strategies to find what resonates best with their unique healing process.

Embracing Growth and Meaning

Resilience can be nurtured by finding purpose and meaning in the midst of grief. Within The Safe Room, individuals are guided to explore ways in which their loss can serve as a catalyst for personal growth. Through activities such as storytelling, legacy projects, and acts of kindness in memory of their loved ones, they discover new sources of purpose and find resilience in the face of adversity.

Exercises for Resilience Building

1. Gratitude Practice

Gratitude exercises, such as keeping a gratitude journal or practicing daily gratitude reflections, help individuals focus on the positive aspects of their lives, fostering resilience by shifting their perspective and cultivating appreciation for what remains.

2. Visualization and Affirmations

Guided visualization exercises and affirmations are powerful tools within The Safe Room to instill a sense of hope, strength, and resilience. Participants are encouraged to create vivid mental images of themselves healing, growing, and embracing life once again.

3. Mindfulness and Self-Awareness

Mindfulness practices, such as body scans, breath awareness, and grounding exercises, allow individuals to cultivate self-awareness and observe their thoughts and emotions without judgment. This practice within The Safe Room helps build resilience by fostering a sense of inner calm and providing a space for self-reflection and growth.

Conclusion:

Empowering individuals to build resilience is a fundamental aspect of The Safe Room's mission to facilitate healing in the face of grief. By recognizing the transformative power of resilience, fostering connections, providing coping strategies, and encouraging the exploration of growth and meaning, The Safe Room offers a roadmap for individuals to navigate their grief journeys with strength and hope. Through exercises that promote self-compassion, gratitude, visualization, mindfulness, and self-awareness, individuals within The Safe Room community are empowered to cultivate resilience, find inner strength, and ultimately embark on a path of healing and thriving.

Empowering Resilience: Nurturing Strength amidst Grief

Within the delicate dance of grief, the emergence of resilience is a testament to the indomitable spirit of the human heart. Chapter 5 of "The Safe Room" delves into the vital importance of Empowering Resilience—an intentional journey toward not just surviving grief but discovering the capacity to thrive in its wake.

The Significance of Resilience in Grief

Grief, by its nature, challenges the very fabric of one's being. Empowering Resilience within The Safe Room is an acknowledgment that, in the face of loss, individuals possess an innate capacity to adapt, grow, and find renewed purpose. This chapter unfolds the significance of resilience as a beacon guiding individuals from the depths of grief toward a future filled with hope.

Strategies to Foster Resilience within the Safe Room

1. Narrative Reconstruction:

- Encourage participants to reframe their grief narratives, emphasizing not only the pain but also the strength and growth that can emerge from adversity.

- Facilitate storytelling sessions within The Safe Room, allowing individuals to share their transformative journeys.

2. Mindfulness and Meditation Practices:

- Introduce mindfulness and meditation exercises to help participants anchor themselves in the present moment.

- Provide guided sessions within The Safe Room, led by experts or through pre-recorded content, focusing on calming techniques and self-awareness.

3. Journaling for Reflection:

- Advocate for the therapeutic practice of journaling to facilitate self-reflection and emotional expression.

- Create dedicated spaces within The Safe Room for individuals to share their journal entries or participate in guided journaling prompts.

4. Building Coping Toolkits

- Collaborate with mental health professionals to compile coping toolkits tailored to different aspects of grief.

- Within The Safe Room, establish resource hubs where participants can explore and create personalized coping strategies that resonate with them.

5. Mind-Body Connection Exercises:

- Offer exercises that emphasize the connection between mental and physical well-being.

- Include activities such as gentle yoga, breathing exercises, or guided relaxation sessions within The Safe Room's repertoire.

6. Gratitude Practices:

- Promote the cultivation of gratitude as a means of shifting focus toward positive aspects of life.

- Implement gratitude challenges or discussions within The Safe Room, encouraging participants to share moments of gratitude amid their grief.

Benefits of Fostering Resilience in the Safe Room

1. Encouraging Personal Growth:

- Empowering resilience within The Safe Room fosters an environment where personal growth becomes an attainable and celebrated outcome of the grief journey.

- Participants discover newfound strengths and capacities they may not have recognized before.

2. Enhancing Emotional Well-Being:

- Resilience-building strategies contribute to the overall emotional well-being of individuals within The Safe Room.

- The Safe Room becomes a space where emotions are acknowledged, processed, and channeled toward growth.

3. Community Support in Resilience:

- The connections forged within The Safe Room amplify the sense of community support in building resilience.

- Participants draw strength not only from their internal resilience but also from the collective resilience of the community.

4. Navigating Future Challenges:

- Resilience equips individuals with tools to navigate future challenges, both within the grief journey and in their broader life experiences.

- The Safe Room becomes a repository of skills and insights that participants can carry forward into various facets of their lives.

Within Resilience, Hope Blossoms

Empowering resilience within The Safe Room is a commitment to nurturing not only the strength to endure but also the courage to thrive. As individuals embark on the journey of building resilience, let this chapter serve as a guide—a reminder that within the challenges of grief lies the potential for transformation, and within resilience, the seeds of hope blossom. Chapter 5 invites participants to not only weather the storm of grief but to emerge stronger, more resilient, and ready to face the future with newfound strength.

CHAPTER 6

RESPONSIVE MODERATION

Within The Safe Room, responsive and supportive moderation plays a vital role in creating a safe and nurturing environment for individuals navigating the complexities of grief. This chapter delves into the significance of moderation within the grief support platform and explores the guidelines and practices followed by moderators to ensure the well-being and cohesion of The Safe Room community.

The Role of Responsive Moderation

Creating a Safe and Inclusive Space

Responsive moderation is essential for fostering a safe and inclusive environment within The Safe Room. Moderators actively monitor discussions, ensuring that all members are treated with respect and empathy. By upholding community guidelines, moderators help create a space where individuals can freely share their experiences, vulnerabilities, and emotions without fear of judgment or harassment.

Facilitating Constructive Communication

Moderators play a crucial role in facilitating constructive and empathetic communication within The Safe Room. They encourage active listening, discourage harmful or triggering language, and intervene when necessary to deescalate conflicts. Through their guidance, moderators promote healthy dialogue and support the growth and healing of community members.

Ensuring Confidentiality and Privacy

Responsive moderation upholds the principles of confidentiality and privacy within The Safe Room. Moderators are entrusted with protecting the personal information shared by community members and ensuring that discussions remain confidential. This fosters trust and encourages individuals to open up and share their stories authentically.

Guidelines and Practices for Moderators

1. Training and Expertise

Moderators within The Safe Room undergo comprehensive training to develop a deep understanding of grief, trauma, and mental health. They possess the knowledge and skills necessary to navigate sensitive conversations and provide appropriate support. Continuous professional development ensures that moderators stay abreast of evolving research and best practices in grief support.

2. Active Listening and Empathy

Responsive moderation emphasizes the importance of active listening and empathy. Moderators attentively engage with community members, validating their experiences, and offering empathetic responses. By demonstrating genuine care and understanding, moderators create a supportive atmosphere that encourages individuals to share their grief openly.

3.Conflict Resolution and Mediation

In cases where conflicts arise within The Safe Room, moderators act as mediators, promoting respectful and constructive dialogue. They address conflicts promptly and impartially, seeking resolution while upholding community guidelines. By fostering a culture of understanding and compassion, moderators help community members navigate disagreements and misunderstandings effectively.

Monitoring for Safety and Well-being

Moderators actively monitor discussions and content within The Safe Room to ensure the safety and well-being of all participants. They exercise vigilance in identifying and addressing potentially harmful or triggering content, providing guidance and support to those in need. Moderators are trained to recognize signs of distress and intervene appropriately, including providing resources and referrals for professional help when necessary.

Cultivating Community Engagement

Responsive moderation encourages active community engagement within The Safe Room. Moderators initiate and participate in discussions, share relevant resources, and facilitate connections among community members. By fostering a sense of belonging and encouraging participation, moderators create an environment where individuals feel supported and valued.

Conclusion:

Responsive moderation is a cornerstone of The Safe Room, ensuring that it remains a safe, inclusive, and supportive space for individuals navigating grief. By creating a safe and nurturing environment, moderators facilitate constructive communication, protect privacy, and uphold community guidelines. Through active listening, empathy, conflict resolution, and vigilant monitoring, moderators play a pivotal role in promoting healing, growth, and resilience within The Safe Room community. Their dedication and expertise create a space where individuals feel heard, understood, and supported on their grief journeys.

In the tender landscape of grief, where vulnerability and emotions intertwine, the role of Responsive Moderation within The Safe Room is paramount. Chapter 6 unveils the significance of this essential element—a commitment to fostering a supportive and secure environment where individuals can freely express their grief and find solace.

The Crucial Role of Responsive Moderation in Grief Support

Grief, by its nature, can evoke a spectrum of emotions and responses. Responsive Moderation within The Safe Room is not just about overseeing discussions; it is a dedication to creating a haven where individuals feel heard, respected, and supported in their unique grief journeys. This chapter explores the multifaceted role of moderation in navigating the delicate balance between openness and safety.

Guidelines and Practices Followed by Moderators in the Safe Room

1. Empathy and Compassion:

- Moderators within The Safe Room are trained to approach every interaction with empathy and compassion.

- They recognize that each individual's grief experience is unique and respond with sensitivity to diverse emotional expressions.

2. Active Listening:

- Responsive Moderation places a premium on active listening. Moderators attentively engage with participants, ensuring that their voices are heard and acknowledged.

- By actively listening, moderators create an atmosphere of trust, where individuals feel valued and understood.

3. Conflict Resolution:

- In the event of conflicts or disagreements within The Safe Room, moderators act as impartial mediators.

- They employ conflict resolution strategies that prioritize understanding and seek to maintain a harmonious and respectful environment.

4. Creating Inclusive Spaces:

- Moderators work to create inclusive spaces where diverse voices are welcomed.

- They actively discourage any form of discrimination, ensuring that The Safe Room remains a space where everyone, regardless of background or experience, can find support.

5. Ensuring Safety:

- The safety and well-being of participants are of utmost importance. Moderators monitor discussions to identify and address any instances of harmful behavior or potential triggers.

- They enforce community guidelines to maintain a safe space for healing.

6. Promoting Constructive Engagement:

- Moderators guide discussions to be constructive and supportive, offering gentle nudges when conversations veer towards negativity.

- They encourage participants to share experiences, insights, and coping strategies that contribute positively to the community.

7. Timely Support and Resources:

 - Responsive Moderation involves providing timely support to participants who may be in distress.

 - Moderators are equipped with resources and information to offer immediate assistance or guide individuals to appropriate help.

Balancing Openness and Safety Within The Safe Room

The Safe Room is not just a space; it is a community that thrives on the delicate balance of openness and safety. Responsive Moderation plays a pivotal role in maintaining this equilibrium, ensuring that individuals can express themselves authentically while feeling secure in their vulnerability.

Community Guidelines and Transparency:

- Moderators adhere to clearly defined community guidelines that prioritize respect, empathy, and inclusivity.

- These guidelines are transparently communicated to participants, fostering a sense of collective responsibility for maintaining a nurturing environment.

Ongoing Training and Development:
- Moderators undergo ongoing training to stay attuned to best practices in grief support and responsive moderation.
- Regular professional development ensures that moderators are well-equipped to handle the evolving needs of The Safe Room community.

In The Safe Room, Moderation is a Guardian of Healing
As individuals share the depths of their grief within The Safe Room, Responsive Moderation stands as a silent guardian, ensuring that the space remains not only open for expression but also a sanctuary of safety. Chapter 6 invites participants to trust in the responsive guidance of moderators, knowing that their grief will be met with understanding, care, and a commitment to the principles that make The Safe Room a haven for healing.

CHAPTER 7

OPEN DIALOGUE

The Importance of Open Dialogue

Grief, with its intricate threads of pain and remembrance, often finds solace in the openness of shared dialogue. Chapter 7 of "The Safe Room" delves into the transformative power of Open Dialogue—a space where individuals are encouraged to express their grief experiences and emotions openly, fostering connection, understanding, and communal healing.

Within The Safe Room, open and honest dialogue serves as a powerful catalyst for healing and growth. This chapter explores the importance of encouraging open dialogue about grief experiences and emotions and highlights the benefits of engaging in such discussions within The Safe Room community.

Breaking the Silence

Grief can often be a topic shrouded in silence, as societal norms and discomfort may discourage open discussions. However, within The Safe Room, open dialogue is actively encouraged. By breaking the silence surrounding grief, individuals are given a safe space to share their experiences, emotions, and challenges. This process provides validation and support, reducing feelings of isolation and promoting healing.

Normalizing Grief Experiences

Open dialogue helps to normalize the wide range of emotions and experiences associated with grief. By sharing their stories, individuals within The Safe Room community realize that their feelings and reactions are valid and shared by others. This normalization reduces self-judgment and fosters self-compassion, allowing individuals to navigate their grief journeys with greater resilience.

Encouraging Emotional Expression

Grief is a deeply emotional experience, and open dialogue provides an outlet for individuals to express and process their emotions. By engaging in honest conversations, individuals can share their sadness, anger, fear, and other complex emotions, allowing for catharsis and emotional release. This emotional expression is essential for healing and finding a sense of peace.

Benefits of Engaging in Open Dialogue

Validation and Belonging

Engaging in open dialogue within The Safe Room community offers a sense of validation and belonging. When individuals hear others share similar experiences and emotions, they realize they are not alone in their grief. This shared understanding creates a supportive atmosphere where individuals feel seen, heard, and accepted, reducing feelings of isolation and fostering connection.

Emotional Support

Open dialogue provides opportunities for individuals to receive emotional support from their peers within The Safe Room community. By sharing their challenges and vulnerabilities, individuals can lean on each other for empathy, compassion, and guidance. The collective wisdom and lived experiences of community members become a source of strength, offering solace and comfort during difficult times.

Perspectives and Insights

Engaging in open dialogue exposes individuals to a diverse range of perspectives and insights. Within The Safe Room, community members come from various backgrounds and have different experiences of grief. By listening to others' stories, individuals gain new perspectives, learn coping strategies, and discover unique approaches to healing. This exposure to diverse perspectives helps expand their own understanding of grief and facilitates personal growth.

Empowerment and Resilience

Open dialogue empowers individuals on their grief journey by providing a space for them to voice their experiences and emotions openly. As they share their stories and receive support, individuals within The Safe Room community build resilience and find strength in their vulnerability. Open dialogue encourages self-reflection, self-compassion, and personal growth, enabling individuals to navigate their grief with courage and hope.

Conclusion:

Open dialogue is a cornerstone of The Safe Room community, fostering healing, connection, and growth. By encouraging individuals to break the silence surrounding grief, open dialogue normalizes experiences, encourages emotional expression, and nurtures a sense of validation and belonging. The benefits of engaging in open dialogue within The Safe Room are numerous, including emotional support, diverse perspectives, personal empowerment, and resilience. Through honest and open conversations, individuals within The Safe Room community find solace, share wisdom, and gain the strength to navigate their grief journeys with grace and resilience.

The Importance of Open and Honest Dialogue in Grief Support

In the journey of grief, words become the threads that weave together the narrative of loss. Open Dialogue within The Safe Room is not just a conversation; it is a collective embrace of vulnerability—a sanctuary where individuals can articulate the depth of their grief without fear of judgment. This chapter explores the profound impact of embracing openness and honesty in navigating the landscapes of grief.

Benefits of Engaging in Open Dialogue Within The Safe Room Community

1. Validation and Normalization:

    - Open Dialogue provides a platform for individuals to share their grief experiences openly.

- Participants realize that their feelings are valid, and the diverse expressions of grief within The Safe Room normalize the spectrum of emotions associated with loss.

2. Fostering Connection and Empathy:

- Through open sharing, participants connect with others who have faced similar experiences.

- Empathy flourishes as individuals find resonance in each other's stories, creating a web of understanding and support.

3. Breaking the Silence of Isolation:

- Grief often brings a sense of isolation. Open Dialogue shatters this silence by encouraging individuals to articulate their feelings and share their stories.

- Participants discover that they are not alone, and their voices contribute to a chorus of shared experiences.

4. Promoting Emotional Release:

- Verbalizing grief is a cathartic process. Open Dialogue provides a safe space for emotional release, allowing individuals to express their pain, anger, or sorrow without inhibition.

- The act of articulating emotions becomes a powerful step in the healing journey.

5. Building a Culture of Support:

- Open Dialogue fosters a culture of mutual support within The Safe Room.

- Participants become not only recipients of empathy but also contributors to a supportive environment where everyone plays a role in the healing process.

6. Encouraging Learning and Growth:

- Through sharing stories and insights, participants gain new perspectives and coping strategies.

- Open Dialogue becomes a platform for collective learning and growth, offering a wealth of experiences and wisdom.

Creating Safe Spaces for Vulnerability

Within The Safe Room, Open Dialogue is more than an invitation to speak—it's a call to be heard, understood, and embraced. The safe spaces cultivated by this openness enable individuals to share the unfiltered truths of their grief, creating an environment where authenticity becomes the foundation of healing.

Guidelines for Open Dialogue Within The Safe Room:

1. Encouraging Respectful Listening:

- Participants are encouraged to actively listen to others, offering respect and empathy.

- The Safe Room community values each person's unique journey, and participants honor this diversity in their responses.

2. Sharing Without Judgment:

- Open Dialogue thrives on the principle of non-judgment.

Participants are reminded to share their experiences without imposing judgments on others.

- Respectful disagreement is embraced, fostering an atmosphere where diverse perspectives coexist.

3. Embracing Vulnerability:

- Open Dialogue celebrates vulnerability as a strength rather than a weakness.

- Participants are empowered to share their raw emotions, knowing that their openness contributes to the collective strength of The Safe Room community.

4. Offering Constructive Feedback:

- Participants are encouraged to provide feedback and insights constructively.

- The Safe Room becomes a space for constructive discussions that uplift and support, fostering an atmosphere of shared growth.

In Open Dialogue, Healing Unfolds

As individuals within The Safe Room engage in Open Dialogue, the words they share become threads in a tapestry—a collective expression of grief that transcends individual experiences. Chapter 7 invites participants to embrace the transformative power of their voices, recognizing that within the open dialogue lies the potential for healing, connection, and the gentle unraveling of the complexities of grief.

CHAPTER 8

OFFERING VALIDATION

Nurturing Hearts through Understanding

In the vast landscape of grief, where emotions unfold like chapters of a poignant story, the act of Offering Validation becomes a cornerstone of healing. Chapter 8 of "The Safe Room" explores the profound significance of acknowledging and understanding the unique experiences of individuals in their grief journey, creating a sanctuary where validation becomes a balm for the wounded heart.

Validation and understanding are essential elements in supporting individuals on their grief journey. This chapter delves into the significance of offering validation and understanding within The Safe Room and provides guidance on how to provide such support effectively.

The Significance of Validation and Understanding

Recognizing the Complexity of Grief

Grief is a deeply personal and complex experience, unique to each individual. Offering validation acknowledges the multifaceted nature of grief and recognizes that there is no "right" or "wrong" way to grieve. By validating individuals' emotions, reactions, and experiences, we affirm their journey and offer them a sense of understanding and acceptance.

Reducing Feelings of Isolation

Grief can be an isolating experience, as individuals often feel like their emotions are misunderstood or trivialized. By offering validation, we let individuals know that their feelings are valid and that they are not alone in their grief. This validation helps create a sense of connection, reducing isolation, and fostering a supportive community within The Safe Room.

Promoting Emotional Healing

Validation plays a crucial role in promoting emotional healing. When individuals feel validated, they experience a sense of relief and acceptance, allowing them to process their emotions and move towards healing. By offering understanding and validation, we create a safe space for individuals to express their grief authentically and find solace in their journey.

Guidance on Offering Validation and Support

1,Practice Active Listening

Active listening is a fundamental aspect of offering validation and support. When engaging in discussions within The Safe Room, give your full attention to the speaker, allowing them to express themselves fully without interruption. Show empathy through nonverbal cues, such as nodding or maintaining eye contact, and ask thoughtful questions to deepen your understanding.

2. Validate Emotions and Experiences

Acknowledge and validate the emotions and experiences expressed by individuals within The Safe Room. Let them know that their feelings are legitimate and understandable. Use phrases like, "I hear you," "Your feelings are valid," or "I can imagine that must be incredibly difficult for you." This validation helps individuals feel seen, heard, and understood.

3. Avoid Judgment and Comparison

In offering validation, it is crucial to refrain from judgment or making comparisons between different grief experiences. Each person's journey is unique, and comparing or dismissing their feelings can invalidate their experiences. Instead, focus on empathy, understanding, and offering support without trying to diminish or trivialize their emotions.

4. Offer Empathetic Responses

Respond with empathy and compassion when individuals share their stories or express their emotions. Reflect back on their feelings and experiences using phrases like, "It sounds like you're feeling..." or "I can understand why that would be so challenging for you." By demonstrating empathy, you create a safe space for individuals to be vulnerable and find comfort within The Safe Room.

5.Encourage Self-Reflection and Self-Compassion

Support individuals in practicing self-reflection and self-compassion. Encourage them to explore their emotions, thoughts, and needs, and remind them to be gentle with themselves throughout their grief journey. Offering guidance on self-care practices and resources within The Safe Room can further empower individuals to navigate their grief with self-compassion and resilience.

Conclusion:

Offering validation and understanding within The Safe Room is essential in supporting individuals on their grief journey. By recognizing the complexity of grief, reducing feelings of isolation, and promoting emotional healing, validation plays a significant role in creating a safe and nurturing environment. By practicing active listening, validating emotions and experiences, avoiding judgment, and offering empathetic responses, we can provide meaningful support to individuals within The Safe Room. Through validation, individuals find solace, connection, and the strength to heal and grow on their unique paths of grief.

The Significance of Offering Validation in the Grief Journey

Grief, with its myriad of emotions, is a deeply personal odyssey. Offering Validation within The Safe Room is an intentional recognition that each person's grief is valid, worthy of acknowledgment, and an integral part of their journey toward healing. This chapter delves into the transformative power of validation in fostering connection, empathy, and a sense of communal understanding.

Guidance on Offering Validation and Support Within The Safe Room

1. Active Listening:

- Actively listen to the words, emotions, and nuances shared by individuals in The Safe Room.

- Demonstrate attentiveness through non-verbal cues such as nodding, eye contact, and reflective responses.

2. Empathetic Responses:

- Respond with empathy and compassion to the expressed feelings of grief.

- Use phrases that convey understanding, such as "I can imagine that must be incredibly difficult" or "Your emotions are valid, and I'm here for you."

3. Avoiding Judgment:

- Cultivate a non-judgmental mindset when engaging in discussions.

- Remind participants that grief is a complex and individual experience, and their feelings are accepted without judgment.

4. Affirming the Validity of Emotions:

- Affirm the legitimacy of the emotions shared by individuals.

- Validate that grief is a nonlinear journey, and there is no "right" or "wrong" way to feel.

5. Sharing Personal Experiences Responsibly:

- When offering validation through personal experiences, do

so responsibly and with the intention of supporting rather than overshadowing the experiences of others.

- Recognize that everyone's grief is unique, and shared stories should enhance understanding rather than diminish individual narratives.

6. Encouraging Self-Validation:

- Guide individuals in recognizing and validating their own emotions.

- Encourage self-compassion and the understanding that their grief is a valid response to loss.

Benefits of Offering Validation Within The Safe Room

1. Fostering a Sense of Belonging:

- Validation creates an environment where individuals feel a sense of belonging within The Safe Room community.

- Participants recognize that their grief is not isolated, and they are part of a compassionate and understanding collective.

2. Diminishing Feelings of Isolation:

- Validating experiences diminish the feelings of isolation that often accompany grief.

- Individuals realize they are not alone in their emotions, and their journey is shared by others within The Safe Room.

3. Enhancing Emotional Well-Being:

- Offering validation contributes to the emotional well-being of individuals.

- Participants feel supported, acknowledged, and empowered to navigate their grief journey with a greater sense of resilience.

4. Building a Culture of Compassion:

- The act of validation contributes to the cultivation of a culture of compassion within The Safe Room.

- Participants learn from one another, offering validation and support in a reciprocal manner that strengthens the fabric of the community.

In Validation, Healing Flourishes

As individuals within The Safe Room extend the gift of validation, they contribute to the collective healing of the community. Chapter 8 invites participants to embrace the transformative power of acknowledging and understanding the grief experiences of others. Within the act of validation, hearts find solace, connection thrives, and the journey of healing becomes a shared endeavor.

CHAPTER 9

MEANINGFUL RITUALS

Creating meaningful rituals to honor and remember loved ones holds significant importance within The Safe Room. This chapter explores the value of such rituals and provides examples and suggestions for incorporating meaningful rituals within The Safe Room community.

The Importance of Meaningful Rituals : Honoring and Remembering Loved Ones

Meaningful rituals provide a way to honor and remember loved ones who have passed away. They offer an opportunity to express love, gratitude, and respect for the impact they had on our lives. Rituals help us maintain a connection with the memories and legacies of those we have lost, keeping their presence alive in our hearts and minds.

Providing a Sense of Continuity

Grief can disrupt our sense of continuity and stability. Meaningful rituals provide a sense of structure and consistency, anchoring us during a time of emotional upheaval. They create a space where we can find solace, reflect on our memories, and find comfort in the familiarity of the rituals themselves.

Facilitating Healing and Closure

Engaging in meaningful rituals can be a healing experience. They provide an opportunity for individuals to express their grief, release emotions, and find closure. Rituals help create a sense of peace and acceptance, allowing individuals to navigate the grieving process and move forward on their journey of healing.

Examples and Suggestions for Meaningful Rituals

1.Remembrance Ceremonies

Organize remembrance ceremonies within The Safe Room community to honor and remember loved ones. These ceremonies can include lighting candles, sharing memories or stories, and offering moments of silence or reflection. By collectively participating in these ceremonies, individuals within The Safe Room community can find solace and support in each other's presence.

2.Virtual Memorials

Create virtual memorials within The Safe Room, dedicated to the memory of loved ones. These memorials can be in the form of dedicated forum threads or shared albums where community members can post photos, stories, and messages. Virtual memorials provide a space for ongoing remembrance and allow individuals to revisit and add to the memories over time.

3.Symbolic Acts

Encourage individuals to engage in symbolic acts that hold significance for them and their loved ones. This can include planting a tree or flowers in their honor, creating artwork or crafts associated with their memory, or writing letters to express unspoken emotions. These symbolic acts provide a tangible way to honor and remember loved ones while fostering individual creativity and healing.

4. Sharing Rituals and Traditions

Within The Safe Room, community members can share their cultural or personal grief rituals and traditions. This exchange of rituals and traditions allows for cross-cultural understanding and provides inspiration for individuals to incorporate meaningful rituals into their own grief journeys. It promotes a sense of unity and learning within the diverse community.

5. Virtual Support Groups

Organize virtual support groups within The Safe Room community, centered around specific themes or aspects of grief. These groups can meet regularly to discuss and engage in meaningful rituals together. Examples include meditation sessions, guided visualization exercises, or journaling prompts designed to foster healing and remembrance.

Conclusion:

Meaningful rituals hold a special place within The Safe Room community, providing opportunities to honor and remember loved ones while fostering healing and closure. By creating a sense of continuity, facilitating healing, and offering a space for remembrance, meaningful rituals contribute to the overall support and well-being of the community. Through remembrance ceremonies, virtual memorials, symbolic acts, sharing of rituals and traditions, and virtual support groups, individuals within The Safe Room find solace, connection, and meaningful ways to navigate their grief journeys while honoring their loved ones' legacies.

In the tapestry of grief, where threads of remembrance weave through the fabric of loss, Chapter 9 of "The Safe Room" illuminates the profound importance of Meaningful Rituals. These rituals, rich with symbolism and intention, serve as bridges between the past and the present, offering a sacred space within The Safe Room to honor and remember loved ones.

The Significance of Creating Meaningful Rituals

Grief often yearns for expression, a tangible manifestation of the love that persists beyond the boundaries of life. Meaningful Rituals within The Safe Room acknowledge that grief is not only about letting go but also about cherishing and commemorating the impact of those we have lost. This chapter explores the depth and significance of rituals as catalysts for healing and remembrance.

Examples and Suggestions for Meaningful Rituals Within The Safe Room Community

1. Virtual Candle Lighting Ceremony:
   - Organize a collective candle lighting ceremony within The Safe Room.
   - Participants can share images or descriptions of candles lit in

honor of their loved ones, creating a virtual space aglow with collective remembrance.

2. Memory Sharing Sessions:

- Host dedicated sessions where individuals share memories of their loved ones.

- These sessions can include stories, anecdotes, or even the sharing of cherished photographs, fostering a sense of shared remembrance.

3. Monthly Commemorative Themes:

- Introduce monthly themes that align with significant dates, seasons, or themes associated with grief and remembrance.

- Participants can engage in activities or discussions related to the theme, creating a rhythm of meaningful rituals throughout the year.

4. Online Memorial Wall:

- Establish a virtual memorial wall within The Safe Room.

- Participants can contribute images, messages, or artworks as a collective tribute to their loved ones, creating a digital sanctuary of shared memories.

5. Guided Reflections and Meditations:

- Offer guided reflections or meditations centered around themes of love, remembrance, and gratitude.

- Participants can engage in these practices collectively or individually, fostering a sense of inner peace and connection.

6. Community Art Projects:

- Initiate collaborative art projects within The Safe Room community.

- Participants can contribute to a collective piece of art, such as a digital collage or virtual scrapbook, expressing their love and memories.

7. Letter-Writing Rituals:

- Encourage participants to write letters to their loved ones.

- These letters can be shared within The Safe Room or kept private, providing a personal and heartfelt means of communication.

8. Seasonal Memorial Gardens:

- Create virtual seasonal memorial gardens within The Safe Room.

- Participants can contribute symbolic elements, such as flowers or icons, representing the changing seasons of grief and remembrance.

Benefits of Meaningful Rituals Within The Safe Room

1. Creating a Sense of Continuity:

- Meaningful rituals provide a sense of continuity and connection with loved ones who have passed.

- Participants find comfort in the regularity of these rituals, creating a rhythm that honors the ongoing relationship with the departed.

2. Fostering Collective Remembrance:

- Rituals within The Safe Room foster a sense of collective remembrance.

- Participants contribute to a shared narrative, where the memories and love for their departed loved ones become part of a larger, interconnected story.

3. Expressing Grief Creatively:

- Rituals offer a creative outlet for expressing grief.

- Participants engage in activities that transcend words, allowing them to channel their emotions into meaningful gestures and creations.

4. Building a Supportive Community:

- Participating in meaningful rituals enhances the sense of community within The Safe Room.

- Shared experiences create bonds, fostering a supportive environment where individuals feel understood and cared for.

In Rituals, Love Echoes Beyond Goodbye

As individuals within The Safe Room embark on the journey of creating and participating in Meaningful Rituals, they engage in a timeless dance of love and remembrance. Chapter 9 invites participants to explore the rich tapestry of grief through intentional acts of ritual, where the echoes of love reverberate beyond the realm of goodbye.

CHAPTER 10

UNDERSTANDING GRIEF

The Nature of Grief

Grief is a complex and deeply personal experience that impacts individuals in various ways. This chapter provides an in-depth exploration of the nature of grief and its effects on individuals. It also examines the different stages and manifestations of grief.

Definition of Grief

Grief is a natural response to loss, encompassing a range of emotional, cognitive, physical, and behavioral reactions. It is not limited to the death of a loved one but can also arise from other significant losses, such as the end of a relationship, the loss of a job, or a major life transition. Grief is a unique and individual process, influenced by personal experiences, beliefs, and cultural factors.

Emotional Impact

Grief elicits a wide range of emotions, including sadness, anger, guilt, anxiety, and numbness. These emotions may fluctuate over time and can be intense and overwhelming. Individuals may experience a sense of emptiness, yearning, or a deep longing for what has been lost. Grief can also bring forth positive emotions, such as gratitude for the time spent with the person who has passed away or a renewed appreciation for life.

Cognitive Impact

Grief can affect an individual's thoughts and cognition. Common cognitive manifestations include difficulty concentrating, memory lapses, confusion, and preoccupation with thoughts of the deceased or the loss. Individuals may also experience questioning of beliefs, spirituality, or existential concerns as they grapple with the meaning and purpose of life in the face of loss.

Physical Impact

Grief can have physical manifestations, such as fatigue, sleep disturbances, changes in appetite, headaches, muscle tension, and a weakened immune system. These physical symptoms can be attributed to the stress response triggered by grief, as well as the emotional and cognitive toll it takes on the individual.

Global and local perspectives

Grief is a universal human experience, but it is also influenced by cultural, social, and personal factors. Therefore, grief in Nigeria and grief in the United States may have some similarities and differences, depending on the context and the individual.

Some possible similarities are:

- Grief is often expressed through emotions, such as sadness, anger, guilt, or numbness.

- Grief is often accompanied by physical symptoms, such as fatigue, insomnia, or pain.

- Grief is often a process that involves different stages or phases, such as denial, anger, bargaining, depression, and acceptance.

- Grief is often influenced by the cause and manner of death, such as natural, accidental, violent, or stigmatized deaths.

- Grief is often a source of spiritual or existential questions, such as the meaning of life, death, and suffering.

Some possible differences are:

- Grief in Nigeria is often more communal and ritualistic, while grief in the United States is often more individualistic and private.

- Grief in Nigeria is often prolonged and complicated by the lack of adequate social support, health care, and legal protection for the bereaved, especially for women and children.

- Grief in Nigeria is often intertwined with traditional African beliefs, such as the existence of ancestors, reincarnation, witchcraft, or curses.

- Grief in the United States is often influenced by the diversity of religious and ethnic backgrounds of the people, as well as the social and economic conditions of the country.

- Grief in the United States is often subject to misconceptions and myths, such as the idea that grief follows a predictable pattern of stages, or that crying is a sign of weakness.

Some statistics that highlight the differences are:

- According to the World Health Organization, the crude death rate (the number of deaths per 1,000 population) in Nigeria was 12.4 in 2019, while in the United States it was 8.9.

- According to the World Bank, the maternal mortality ratio (the number of maternal deaths per 100,000 live births) in Nigeria was 917 in 2017, while in the United States it was 19.

- According to the Global Terrorism Database, the number of terrorist attacks in Nigeria was 1,549 in 2019, resulting in 2,043 deaths and 1,118 injuries, while in the United States it was 57, resulting in 5 deaths and 24 injuries.

- According to the U.S. Census Bureau, the percentage of foreign-born population in the United States was 13.7% in 2019, representing various countries, regions, and religions, while in Nigeria it was 0.6%, mostly from neighboring African countries.

- In Nigeria, a woman who lost her husband and three children in a terrorist attack said, "I have no one left. I don't know how to live. I don't know where to go. I don't know what to do. I wish I had died with them."

- In the United States, a man who lost his wife and daughter in a car accident said, "I feel like I'm in a fog. I can't concentrate. I can't sleep. I can't eat. I can't work. I can't function. I feel guilty for being alive."

Here's a mnemonic using the word "SAFE ROOM" to represent different aspects of providing support for grief and healing:

S - Sympathetic Listening: Offering empathetic and compassionate listening to individuals in grief.

A - Accessible Resources: Providing easily accessible resources and information for grief support.

F - Facilitating Connections: Facilitating connections between individuals who have experienced similar grief.

E - Empowering Resilience: Empowering individuals to build resilience and cope with their grief.

R - Responsive Moderation: Ensuring responsive and supportive moderation within the grief support platform.

O - Open Dialogue: Encouraging open and honest dialogue about grief experiences and emotions.

O - Offering Validation: Offering validation and understanding to individuals in their grief journey.

M - Meaningful Rituals: Encouraging the creation of meaningful rituals to honor and remember loved ones.

The science of grief

Anatomy of grief

The exploration of the anatomy of grief encompasses various dimensions and experiences that together form the intricate process of grieving. While grief is a deeply personal and individual journey, there are common elements and stages that many people go through when faced with the loss of a loved one or significant life changes. Let us delve into some key aspects of this intricate anatomy:

1. Emotional Response: Grief often evokes a range of intense emotions, such as profound sadness, anger, guilt, confusion, and despair. These feelings can arise in unpredictable waves and may fluctuate over time, making the grieving experience all the more complex.

2. Physical Sensations: Grief can manifest in physical ways, impacting the body. It may bring about sensations like fatigue, a

tightness in the chest, shortness of breath, loss of appetite, sleep disturbances, and an overall sense of heaviness or emptiness.

3. Cognitive Impact: Grief can affect our thinking patterns and cognitive functioning. It may lead to difficulties with concentration, memory lapses, a preoccupation with the loss, and a sense of disbelief or confusion as we try to make sense of our new reality.

4. Social and Behavioral Changes: Grief often prompts changes in our social interactions and behavior. Some individuals may withdraw from social activities, lose interest in previously enjoyed pursuits, or struggle to connect with others. Conversely, some individuals may actively seek support and connection as they navigate their grief.

5. Spiritual and Existential Reflection: The experience of grief often sparks contemplation of life's meaning, mortality, and our place in the world. It can inspire a search for deeper understanding, spiritual exploration, and reflection on existential themes as we grapple with the profound questions that arise.

6. Coping Mechanisms: People employ various coping mechanisms to navigate their grief. These can include seeking support from others, engaging in self-care activities, finding solace in spiritual or religious practices, or expressing emotions through creative outlets such as art or writing.

7. Stages of Grief: While not everyone experiences grief in a linear

or predictable manner, the Kübler-Ross model outlines five common stages of grief: denial, anger, bargaining, depression, and acceptance. These stages provide a framework for understanding the emotional journey that individuals may traverse as they process their loss.

Physiology of grief

The physiology of grief refers to the physical and biological changes that occur in the body in response to the experience of grief. Grief can have a profound impact on various physiological processes, as well as on the overall well-being of an individual. Here are some key aspects of the physiology of grief:

1. Stress Response: Grief triggers a significant stress response in the body. When a person experiences loss, the body releases stress hormones such as cortisol and adrenaline. These hormones can lead to physiological changes, including increased heart rate, elevated blood pressure, and heightened alertness.

2. Immune System: Grief can affect the functioning of the immune system. Studies have shown that individuals experiencing grief may have altered immune responses, making them more susceptible to infections and illnesses. The stress associated with grief can weaken the immune system's ability to fight off pathogens effectively.

3. Sleep Disturbances: Grief often disrupts sleep patterns. Many individuals experiencing grief may struggle with insomnia,

difficulty falling asleep, or disrupted sleep throughout the night. Sleep disturbances can further impact overall physical health and emotional well-being.

4. Appetite and Digestion: Grief can affect appetite and digestion. Some individuals may experience a loss of appetite, leading to weight loss and nutritional deficiencies. Others may turn to food for comfort, resulting in weight gain or unhealthy eating patterns. Changes in the digestive system can also lead to gastrointestinal symptoms such as stomachaches or digestive discomfort.

5. Energy Levels and Fatigue: Grief can be physically exhausting. The emotional toll of grief, combined with the stress response in the body, can lead to feelings of fatigue and low energy levels. Individuals may find it challenging to engage in daily activities or experience a lack of motivation.

6. Neurotransmitters and Mood: Grief can impact the balance of neurotransmitters in the brain, which play a crucial role in regulating mood. Serotonin, for example, is often associated with feelings of well-being and happiness. The disruption of neurotransmitter levels during grief can contribute to symptoms of depression, anxiety, and mood swings.

7. Heart Health: The stress associated with grief can have implications for heart health. Studies have shown that individuals experiencing grief may have an increased risk of cardiovascular

events, such as heart attacks or irregular heart rhythms. The physiological changes during grief, including elevated blood pressure and heart rate, can place additional strain on the cardiovascular system.

It's important to recognize that the physiological responses to grief can vary among individuals. Some people may experience these changes more acutely and for a longer duration, while others may have a less pronounced physiological response. Taking care of one's physical well-being through healthy lifestyle choices, seeking support, and engaging in self-care activities can help mitigate the physiological impact of grief and support overall healing.

Biochemistry of grief

The biochemistry of grief refers to the chemical changes that occur in the body at a molecular level in response to the experience of grief. Grief can influence various biochemical processes, including neurotransmitter levels, hormone regulation, and immune system functioning. Here are some key aspects of the biochemistry of grief:

1. Neurotransmitters: Grief can affect the balance of neurotransmitters in the brain, which are chemical messengers responsible for transmitting signals between brain cells. Serotonin, dopamine, and norepinephrine are among the neurotransmitters that play a role in regulating mood and emotions. Grief can disrupt the normal levels and functioning of these neurotransmitters, leading to symptoms such as depression, anxiety, and mood swings.

2. Stress Hormones: Grief triggers the release of stress hormones, such as cortisol and adrenaline, in the body. These hormones are part of the body's physiological stress response and help mobilize energy and increase alertness. However, prolonged or excessive release of stress hormones due to grief can have negative effects on physical and mental well-being, including increased risk of cardiovascular problems, impaired immune function, and disrupted sleep patterns.

3. Inflammatory Response: Grief can also influence the body's inflammatory response. Studies have shown that prolonged or chronic grief can lead to increased levels of pro-inflammatory markers in the body. Inflammation is a natural process that helps the body fight off infections and heal from injuries, but excessive or prolonged inflammation can contribute to various health issues, including cardiovascular disease, autoimmune disorders, and mental health problems.

4. Immune System: Grief can impact immune system functioning. The stress associated with grief can suppress immune responses, making individuals more susceptible to infections and illnesses. Additionally, grief-related changes in cortisol levels can affect immune cells and their ability to defend against pathogens. This can result in increased vulnerability to infections and a slower healing process.

5. Endorphins and Opioids: Grief can influence the release of endorphins and other opioids in the body. These natural chemicals

are associated with feelings of comfort, pain relief, and a sense of well-being. During the grieving process, the body may produce endorphins as a coping mechanism to help alleviate emotional and physical pain.

6. Sleep Regulation: Grief can disrupt sleep patterns and influence the regulation of sleep-related hormones, such as melatonin. Insomnia and sleep disturbances are common during grief, which can further impact overall physical and emotional well-being.

It's important to note that the biochemistry of grief is complex, and individual responses may vary. Factors such as the type and intensity of the loss, personal coping mechanisms, and overall health can influence the biochemical changes experienced during grief. Seeking support, engaging in self-care activities, and maintaining a healthy lifestyle can help support the body's biochemistry during the grieving process.

Psychology of Grief

The psychology of grief refers to the psychological and emotional processes that individuals experience when they are confronted with loss. Grief is a complex and individualized experience that can impact various aspects of a person's psychological well-being. Here are some key elements of the psychology of grief:

1. Emotional Response: Grief is often accompanied by a wide range of intense emotions. These may include sadness, anger, guilt,

confusion, shock, disbelief, loneliness, and anxiety. These emotions can come in waves and may fluctuate in intensity over time.

2. Denial and Disbelief: Initially, individuals may experience a sense of denial or disbelief when faced with a significant loss. It can be challenging to accept the reality of the loss, leading to a period of shock or numbness.

3. Anger and Resentment: Grief can evoke feelings of anger and resentment. Individuals may direct their anger towards themselves, the deceased, others involved in the situation, or even a higher power. These emotions can be a normal part of the grieving process, and it's important to find healthy ways to express and manage them.

4. Bargaining and Guilt: During grief, individuals may engage in bargaining or experience feelings of guilt. They might find themselves attempting to negotiate with a higher power or questioning their own actions and decisions leading up to the loss. This can be accompanied by a sense of guilt or self-blame.

5. Depression and Sadness: Grief often involves a period of depression and profound sadness. Individuals may feel a deep sense of loss, emptiness, and a lack of interest in activities they once enjoyed. It's important to distinguish between normal grief-related sadness and clinical depression. If depressive symptoms persist and significantly impair daily functioning, seeking professional help is advisable.

6. Acceptance and Meaning-Making: As individuals progress through the grieving process, they may gradually come to accept the reality of the loss. Acceptance doesn't mean forgetting or moving on from the loss, but rather integrating it into one's life and finding ways to move forward. Many people also engage in meaning-making, seeking to find or create meaning from the loss and understand how it fits into their personal narrative.

7. Individual Differences: It's important to recognize that grief is a highly individual experience, and there is no "right" or "wrong" way to grieve. People differ in their coping styles, cultural backgrounds, and personal beliefs, all of which can influence the psychological response to grief. Some individuals may seek social support and openly express their emotions, while others may prefer a more private and introspective approach.

8. Grief and Identity: Grief can impact an individual's sense of identity. The loss of a loved one or a significant life change can challenge one's self-concept and lead to questioning of personal values, beliefs, and life goals. Reconstructing a sense of self and navigating identity-related changes is an integral part of the grief process.

It's important to remember that grief is a highly individual and non-linear process. The psychological aspects of grief can be complex and may vary from person to person. Seeking support from loved ones, joining support groups, or seeking professional counseling can be valuable resources for navigating the psychological challenges of grief.

The Dynamic Stages of Grief:

Grief is not confined to the realm of death and dying alone; it extends to significant changes or losses in life. Kübler-Ross outlined five stages commonly observed in the grieving process: denial, anger, bargaining, depression, and acceptance. These stages, represented by the acronym DABDA, provide a general guide rather than a rigid rule. However, it is crucial to recognize that these stages are not linear, nor are they experienced uniformly by all individuals.

The Kübler-Ross Model

Grief, a universal human experience, manifests in various forms throughout our lives. Dr. Elisabeth Kübler-Ross, a Swiss psychiatrist, introduced the well-known Kübler-Ross model in her influential book "On Death and Dying." Initially developed from her work with terminally ill patients, encompassing five stages of grief from denial to acceptance. However, this model has faced criticism for its perceived linearity and applicability. In this exploration of grief, we delve beyond Kübler-Ross' framework and acknowledge the multifaceted nature of this complex emotion.

In 1969, Elisabeth Kübler-Ross described five common stages of grief, popularly referred to as DABDA. They include:

Denial: The initial stage of grief, where one may resist accepting the reality of their loss or impending death. Denial can serve as a protective mechanism, allowing individuals to cope with the initial shock and overwhelming emotions.

Anger: As grief intensifies, anger may arise. Individuals may direct their rage and resentment toward the situation, themselves, or others. This stage provides an outlet for expressing pent-up emotions and confronting the pain of loss.

Bargaining: In an attempt to regain control or seek meaning, individuals may enter the bargaining stage. They may negotiate with a higher power, fate, or themselves, hoping to postpone or reverse the outcome. This stage offers a temporary sense of empowerment and purpose.

Depression: As reality sets in, a profound sense of sadness, hopelessness, and despair may engulf individuals in the depression stage. Withdrawal, loss of interest in activities, and physical symptoms may manifest. This stage allows for introspection and emotional processing.

Acceptance: The final stage of grief, acceptance, involves coming to terms with the reality of the situation and embracing it. It allows individuals to find peace, calmness, and a renewed sense of purpose. Acceptance does not imply forgetting or moving on swiftly; it signifies an acknowledgment of the loss and the beginning of a new chapter.

Beyond the Kübler-Ross Model: Embracing Complexity:
Denial, the initial stage of grief, serves as a temporary shield that

helps us navigate the overwhelming impact of loss. During this stage, life may appear devoid of meaning, leaving us feeling disoriented and burdened. We may find ourselves denying the news, essentially numbing our emotions.

In this phase, it is common to question how life can continue in this altered state. When faced with a life-threatening illness, one might doubt the accuracy of the diagnosis, speculating that a laboratory error occurred or their test results got mixed up with someone else's. Similarly, upon receiving news of a loved one's death, it is natural to cling to the hope that there has been a mistaken identification. During the denial stage, we create a "preferable" version of reality rather than accepting the harsh truth of the situation.

Surprisingly, denial and shock play a vital role in helping us cope and endure the initial impact of grief. Denial acts as a buffer, allowing us to pace our emotional response to the loss. By denying and not fully accepting the grief, we prevent ourselves from being completely overwhelmed. This can be seen as a protective mechanism, a natural defense mechanism of our body saying, "I can only handle so much at once."

It is important to recognize that while denial may offer temporary solace, it is not a sustainable state. As we move through the grieving process, it becomes essential to face the reality of the loss and begin the journey towards healing and acceptance. Denial, though initially helpful, must eventually give way to a deeper exploration of our emotions in order to truly honor and process our grief.

Anger

As you gradually return to living in the realm of "actual" reality, anger may begin to surface. It is common during this stage to question, "Why me?" and exclaim, "Life's not fair!" You may find yourself seeking someone or something to blame for the cause of your grief, even directing your anger towards close friends and family. It becomes incomprehensible to understand why such a situation has befallen you. For those with strong faith, this stage may involve questioning their belief in God and asking, "Where is God? Why didn't he protect me?"

Both researchers and mental health professionals recognize anger as an essential part of the grieving process. They encourage acknowledging and fully experiencing this anger. It is crucial to allow yourself to truly feel the anger, as suppressing it can hinder the healing journey. Although it may seem like an endless cycle, the more you genuinely experience your anger, the faster it will dissipate, leading to a swifter healing process. It is important to note that suppressing anger is not healthy; it is a natural response and, arguably, a necessary one.

However, while it is advised not to suppress anger, it is equally important not to let it control you. If you find it challenging to process your anger, seeking help from a trained counselor or therapist can be beneficial.

In our daily lives, we are often encouraged to control our anger towards situations and others. When faced with a grief event, you may feel disconnected from reality, as if there is no solid ground to hold onto. Your life may seem shattered, leaving you without a firm foundation. Consider anger as a strength that anchors you to reality. During a grief event, you may experience feelings of desertion and abandonment, perceiving yourself as alone in the world. Directing your anger towards something or someone can serve as a bridge back to reality and reconnect you with people. It becomes a tangible "thing" to grasp onto, a natural step in the healing process.

Bargaining

When faced with adversity, have you ever found yourself struck by the impulse to strike a deal with a higher power? Perhaps you pleaded, "Please God, if you heal my husband, I promise to be the best wife I can be and never complain again." This is known as bargaining.

In a way, this stage embraces false hope. It is a form of self-deception, a belief that you can somehow sidestep grief through negotiation. You convince yourself that by making a significant life change, you can restore your existence to the way it was before the event that caused your grief.

Bargaining often goes hand in hand with guilt. It is during this time that a relentless string of "what ifs" may plague your thoughts. What if you had left the house a few minutes earlier? The accident might never have occurred. What if you had encouraged your partner to see the doctor six months ago, as you initially thought? Perhaps the cancer could have been detected earlier, and their life could have been saved.

Depression

Depression, a common companion of grief, can be a reaction to the profound emptiness experienced when confronting the reality that the person or situation is no longer present. During this stage, you may withdraw from life, feeling numb and trapped in a fog. Getting out of bed might seem like an insurmountable task, and the world may appear overwhelming. You might prefer solitude, avoiding contact with others and experiencing a sense of hopelessness. In some cases, these feelings can even lead to thoughts of ending one's own life, as the question of "What's the point of going on?" pervades your mind.

Acceptance

The final stage of grief, as identified by Kübler-Ross, is acceptance. However, acceptance does not imply that you are okay with the loss itself, such as saying, "It's okay that my husband died." Rather, it signifies a recognition that the loss has occurred and that you will find a way to move forward despite it.

During this stage, your emotions may begin to stabilize, and you gradually re-engage with reality. You come to terms with the fact that your loved one will not return or that your illness may inevitably progress. It is not a "good" thing per se, but it is a starting point from which you can rebuild your life.

This stage necessitates constant adjustment and readjustment. There will be good days and bad days, and then there will be good days again. Acceptance does not mean that you will never experience another day of overwhelming sadness. However, the positive moments tend to outweigh the negative ones.

In this stage, you may emerge from the fog, reconnect with friends, and even form new relationships over time. You understand that your loved one can never be replaced, but you find ways to move forward, grow, and adapt to your new reality.

It is essential to recognize that grief does not adhere to a predetermined path or timeline. Each individual's experience is unique. Some may not experience all the stages, while others may undergo only a few. The Kübler-Ross model, though widely observed, does not capture the full range of grief experiences.

As we navigate the complexities of grief, it is crucial to approach each person's journey with empathy, understanding, and respect. Grief is a deeply personal and transformative process, and it is our responsibility to support and honor the diverse ways individuals grieve.

Conclusion:

Grief, a profound and universal human experience, defies easy categorization. While the Kübler-Ross model provides a valuable framework, it is essential to move beyond its limitations. We must acknowledge that grief is complex, varied, and deeply personal. As we extend compassion and support to those navigating grief, let us remember the words of renowned author and poet Maya Angelou: "We delight in the beauty of the butterfly but rarely admit the changes it has gone through to achieve that beauty." May we honor the transformative power of grief and embrace the strength and resilience it engenders in us all.

It is important to acknowledge that grief is an intensely personal experience, and each person may navigate it in their own unique way. There is no "right" or "wrong" way to grieve, and individuals may encounter different aspects of grief at various times and with differing intensities. Granting oneself time, space, and support to navigate the complexities of grief and find healing in one's own way is crucial.

Theories explaining grief

There are many theories and models that try to explain how people cope with grief and loss. Here are five of the most well-known ones:

- The five stages of grief: This theory, proposed by psychiatrist Elisabeth Kübler-Ross, suggests that people go through five distinct stages after a loss: denial, anger, bargaining, depression, and acceptance. These stages are not linear or sequential, and people may experience them differently or not at all.

- The dual process model of grief: This model, developed by psychologists Margaret Stroebe and Henk Schut, proposes that grief involves two types of processes: loss-oriented and restoration-oriented. Loss-oriented processes focus on the loss itself, such as remembering the person who died or feeling the pain of separation. Restoration-oriented processes focus on adapting to the new situation, such as finding new roles, activities, or relationships, or making changes in life. People may switch between the two types of processes, depending on their needs and circumstances.

- Tonkin's model of grief: This model, created by grief counselor Lois Tonkin, describes grief as a process of "growing around the grief". According to this model, in the initial stages of bereavement, grief tends to be all-consuming. As time goes on, the grief remains, but instead of consuming a person's entire world, the grief grows smaller, and other areas of the person's life grow larger.

- Meaning reconstruction theory: This theory, based on the work of psychologist Robert Neimeyer, suggests that grief is a process of finding or creating meaning in the face of loss. People may try to make sense of why the loss happened, what it means for their identity and worldview, and how they can continue to live with purpose and hope. Meaning reconstruction can involve telling stories, expressing emotions, or engaging in rituals or practices that honor the person who died.

- **Disenfranchised grief:** This concept, coined by sociologist Kenneth Doka, refers to grief that is not acknowledged or supported by society. This can happen when the loss is not recognized as significant, such as the death of a pet, a friend, or an ex-partner, or when the relationship is stigmatized, such as in cases of suicide, abortion, or infidelity. People who experience disenfranchised grief may feel isolated, invalidated, or ashamed of their feelings.

These are just some of the ways to understand grief and loss, and how they affect people. There are many other theories, perspectives, and experiences that can enrich our knowledge and empathy on this topic.

Conclusion:

Ultimately, the essence of the safe room lies in the transformation of our collective consciousness. It calls us to transcend self-interest and cultivate a genuine concern for the well-being of others. By embodying the teachings of the Igbo adage, we create a ripple effect of empathy, compassion, and unity that extends far beyond the safe room itself.

As we embrace the wisdom of this adage, let us strive to build safe rooms in our communities, workplaces, and relationships. Let us foster environments where the burdens of others are shared, and their suffering is met with understanding and kindness. In doing so, we tap into the depths of our humanity and contribute to a world where empathy and compassion prevail.That is the true essence of the Safe Room!

Manifestations of Grief

Grief can manifest in various ways, and individuals may experience a combination of these manifestations:

- Emotional Manifestations: Intense sadness, anger, guilt, anxiety, fear, numbness, and a wide range of other emotions.

- Cognitive Manifestations: Difficulty concentrating, memory lapses, confusion, intrusive thoughts, and questioning of beliefs.

- Physical Manifestations: Fatigue, sleep disturbances, changes in appetite, headaches, gastrointestinal issues, and weakened immune system.

- Behavioral Manifestations: Social withdrawal, loss of interest in activities, changes in daily routines, restlessness, and increased sensitivity to reminders of the loss.

Individual Differences in Grief

It is important to recognize that grief is a deeply personal experience, and individuals may experience it differently. Factors such as personality, coping mechanisms, past experiences with loss, cultural background, and available support systems can influence how grief is expressed and processed. There is no "right" or "wrong" way to grieve, and it is essential to honor and respect each individual's unique grief journey.

Conclusion:

Grief is a complex and multifaceted experience that encompasses emotional, cognitive, physical, and behavioral manifestations. Understanding the nature of grief and its impact on individuals is crucial in providing support and empathy within The Safe Room community. The stages of grief, as outlined in the Kübler-Ross model, offer a framework for understanding the emotional process individuals may go through. However, it is essential to remember that grief is highly individual, and each person's journey will be unique. By acknowledging the diverse manifestations of grief and supporting one another with empathy and compassion, The Safe Room community can provide a nurturing environment for individuals to navigate their grief and find healing and solace.

In the quiet spaces of the heart, grief unfolds as a poignant and intricate tapestry, weaving through the threads of love, remembrance, and profound loss. Chapter 10 of "The Safe Room" delves into the profound exploration of Understanding Grief—a journey through the multifaceted nature of sorrow, its varied stages, and the intricate manifestations that shape the landscape of individual grief experiences.

The Nature of Grief: A Complex Tapestry

Grief is an emotion both universal and intensely personal. At its core, grief is a response to loss, a reaction to the profound absence of someone or something deeply cherished. Within The Safe Room, we embark on an exploration of the nature of grief, acknowledging its complexity and the unique journey each individual undertakes.

Stages of Grief: A Fluid Journey

1. Denial and Shock:
    - In the initial stage, individuals may experience a sense of disbelief and shock, struggling to comprehend the reality of the loss.
    - Emotions may include numbness, confusion, and an instinct to resist the truth.

2. Anger and Guilt:

- As the reality of the loss settles, anger and guilt may surface.

- Individuals might direct anger toward themselves, others, or even the departed loved one. Guilt may arise from perceived responsibilities or unresolved emotions.

3. Bargaining:

- The bargaining stage involves a quest for understanding and reconciliation.

- Individuals may find themselves negotiating with a higher power or attempting to make sense of the circumstances surrounding the loss.

4. Depression:

- Depression in grief is a profound sadness and a sense of emotional heaviness.

- It may manifest as feelings of deep sorrow, isolation, and an overwhelming sense of emptiness.

5. Acceptance and Integration:

- Acceptance is not about forgetting or moving on but about integrating the loss into one's life.

- This stage involves finding a new normal, where the memories of the departed become a cherished part of the individual's narrative.

Manifestations of Grief: A Kaleidoscope of Emotions

1. Emotional Manifestations:

- Grief manifests as a spectrum of emotions, from intense sadness and longing to moments of anger, confusion, or even relief.

- Emotional expressions vary widely among individuals and may change over time.

2. Physical Manifestations:

- Grief can have physical manifestations, including fatigue, changes in appetite, insomnia, or even physical pain.

- These physical symptoms are often intertwined with the emotional toll of grief.

3. Cognitive Manifestations:

- Grief may affect cognitive processes, leading to difficulties in concentration, memory lapses, or a sense of detachment from reality.

- These cognitive manifestations are part of the mind's complex response to loss.

4. Behavioral Manifestations:

- Grief influences behavior, prompting individuals to withdraw, seek solitude, or, conversely, seek increased social connections.

- Behavioral responses may fluctuate as individuals navigate the ebb and flow of grief.

Individualized Grief Journeys: Navigating the Uncharted
Within The Safe Room, we recognize that grief is not a linear path but an individualized journey, as unique as the relationships and

losses it encompasses. Each person's experience of grief is a mosaic of emotions, stages, and manifestations that evolve over time.

Guiding Principles Within The Safe Room:

1. Non-Judgmental Understanding:

- The Safe Room fosters an environment of non-judgmental understanding, recognizing that grief is deeply personal and diverse.

- Participants are encouraged to share their experiences without fear of comparison or criticism.

2. Validation of Emotions:

- Emotions experienced within grief are valid, irrespective of their nature.

- The Safe Room provides a space where individuals can articulate and validate their emotions, fostering a sense of acceptance.

3. Supportive Community:

- The Safe Room community serves as a support network, acknowledging that grief can be isolating.

- Participants find solace in the shared experiences and understanding within the community.

In Understanding Grief, Compassion Unfolds

As individuals within The Safe Room navigate the complex landscape of grief, Chapter 10 invites them to explore the depths of their emotions, recognizing that understanding grief is an ongoing process. Here, within the pages of this sanctuary, we embrace the diverse nature of grief, offering compassion, understanding, and a guiding light through the uncharted territories of sorrow.

COPING STRATEGIES

In the intricate dance of grief, coping strategies become the steady anchors that help individuals weather the storm of emotional distress. Chapter 11 of "The Safe Room" unveils a spectrum of Coping Strategies—tools and techniques designed to guide individuals through the turbulent seas of grief, offering solace, resilience, and a pathway toward healing.

Introduction to Coping Strategies in Grief

Grief is an emotional landscape marked by peaks and valleys, and coping strategies serve as essential companions on this journey. Whether navigating the tumultuous waves of sadness or finding moments of calm amidst the storm, these strategies empower individuals to confront the complexities of grief with resilience and compassion.

Various Coping Strategies: A Compass for Healing

1. Expressive Writing:

   - Encourage individuals to engage in expressive writing as a therapeutic outlet.

   - The act of putting emotions into words can be cathartic, providing a channel for processing and releasing grief.

2. Mindfulness and Meditation:

- Introduce mindfulness and meditation practices to cultivate a present-focused awareness.

- Techniques such as deep breathing or guided meditation can offer moments of peace and centering.

3. Art and Creativity:

- Explore the healing power of artistic expression.

- Participants can engage in art, music, or other creative pursuits as a means of self-expression and a way to honor their emotions.

4. Support Groups and Connections:

- Emphasize the importance of seeking support from like-minded individuals.

- Joining support groups, either within The Safe Room or in local communities, provides a sense of belonging and shared understanding.

5. Physical Exercise:

- Highlight the benefits of physical activity in managing grief.

- Regular exercise not only contributes to physical well-being but also releases endorphins, promoting a positive outlook.

6. Mind-Body Techniques:

- Explore mind-body techniques such as yoga or tai chi.

- These practices integrate physical movement with mindfulness, fostering a holistic approach to coping with grief.

7. Grief Counseling and Therapy:

- Encourage individuals to seek professional help when needed.

- Grief counseling or therapy, whether in person or online, provides a structured and supportive environment for processing emotions.

8. Journaling and Reflection:

- Advocate for the therapeutic benefits of journaling.

- Participants can use journals to reflect on their grief journey, track progress, and explore personal insights.

Resources and Techniques Within The Safe Room

1. Guided Coping Sessions:

- Host guided coping sessions within The Safe Room, offering participants structured support.

- Trained facilitators or moderators can lead sessions focusing on specific coping techniques.

2. Resource Library:

- Establish a comprehensive resource library within The Safe Room.

- Curate materials, articles, and videos that provide information on coping strategies, allowing participants to explore a variety of approaches.

3. Virtual Workshops:

- Arrange virtual workshops featuring experts in grief counseling and coping techniques.

- These workshops provide a platform for participants to learn and interact with professionals within The Safe Room community.

4. Interactive Challenges:

- Create interactive challenges centered around coping strategies.

- Participants can engage in challenges designed to encourage the practice of coping techniques, fostering a sense of community participation.

5. Peer Support Matching:

- Implement a peer support matching system within The Safe Room.

- Individuals can connect with peers who share similar grief experiences, providing mutual support and encouragement.

Empowering Through Coping Strategies: A Guiding Light

As individuals within The Safe Room explore the vast array of coping strategies, Chapter 11 invites them to embrace the diversity of approaches available. Coping strategies are not one-size-fits-all; instead, they serve as a compass, guiding individuals toward the strategies that resonate most profoundly with their unique journey. Here, within the sanctuary of The Safe Room, coping becomes a shared endeavor, a source of strength, and a pathway to resilience in the face of grief's tumultuous seas.

Coping with grief and emotional distress is a challenging but essential part of the healing process. This chapter introduces various coping strategies that can help individuals manage their grief and navigate emotional distress. It also highlights specific resources and techniques available within The Safe Room community.

Coping Strategies for Grief and Emotional Distress

Self-Care Practices

Engaging in self-care activities is crucial for managing grief and emotional distress. This can include ensuring adequate rest and sleep, maintaining a nutritious diet, engaging in regular exercise, and practicing relaxation techniques such as deep breathing, meditation, or mindfulness. Self-care allows individuals to nurture their physical and emotional well-being, providing a foundation for healing.

Seeking Support

Seeking support from others is an essential coping strategy. This can involve reaching out to friends, family, or support groups within The Safe Room community. Sharing one's feelings and experiences with trusted individuals can provide comfort, validation, and a sense of connection. The Safe Room community offers a supportive environment where individuals can find understanding and empathy from others who have experienced similar losses.

Expressive Writing

Writing can be a powerful tool for processing emotions and gaining clarity. Encourage individuals within The Safe Room community to engage in expressive writing, such as journaling or writing letters to their deceased loved ones. This practice allows for the expression of thoughts, feelings, and memories, fostering emotional release and promoting self-reflection.

Creative Outlets

Engaging in creative activities can be therapeutic and provide an outlet for emotions. Encourage individuals to explore creative outlets such as painting, drawing, music, or poetry. These forms of expression can help individuals channel their emotions, find meaning in their grief, and create something tangible that honors their loved ones' memory.

Mindfulness and Meditation

Practicing mindfulness and meditation techniques can help individuals cultivate present-moment awareness and manage overwhelming emotions. Encourage The Safe Room community members to participate in guided meditations or mindfulness exercises that focus on acceptance, self-compassion, and non-judgment. These practices can bring a sense of calm and provide a space for individuals to observe and process their thoughts and emotions.

Resources and Techniques within The Safe Room

Support Groups and Forums

The Safe Room community offers support groups and forums where individuals can connect with others who have experienced loss. These platforms provide a safe space for sharing stories, seeking advice, and offering support. By participating in these groups, individuals can gain insights, find solace, and learn coping strategies from others who are on a similar journey.

Virtual Workshops and Webinars

The Safe Room community organizes virtual workshops and webinars on various topics related to grief and coping strategies. These educational resources offer valuable insights and practical tools for managing grief and emotional distress. Topics may include mindfulness practices, self-care techniques, creative expression, and navigating the different stages of grief.

Resource Library

The Safe Room's resource library is a collection of articles, books, and other materials that provide guidance and support for individuals experiencing grief. The library offers a wealth of information on coping strategies, self-help techniques, and professional advice. Community members can access these resources to deepen their understanding of grief and explore additional coping strategies.

Conclusion:

Coping with grief and emotional distress requires intentional effort and support. By incorporating coping strategies such as self-care practices, seeking support, expressive writing, creative outlets, and mindfulness techniques, individuals within The Safe Room community can develop resilience and find healing amidst their grief. The community itself provides valuable resources, including support groups, virtual workshops, and a comprehensive resource library. By actively engaging with these resources and techniques, individuals can navigate their grief journeys with greater strength, self-awareness, and a sense of belonging within The Safe Room community.

CHAPTER 12

SEEKING PROFESSIONAL HELP

Seeking professional help is an important step in the healing journey of grief and emotional distress. This chapter discusses the role of professional counselors and therapists in supporting individuals through their grief. It also provides guidance on how to find appropriate professional help and highlights the resources available within The Safe Room community.

The Role of Professional Counselors and Therapists

Professional Expertise

Professional counselors and therapists are trained professionals who specialize in providing support and guidance to individuals experiencing grief and emotional distress. They possess the knowledge and skills to help individuals navigate complex emotions, develop coping strategies, and facilitate healing. Their expertise can provide valuable insights and tools for individuals on their grief journeys.

Emotional Support and Validation

Counselors and therapists create a safe and non-judgmental space where individuals can express their emotions, thoughts, and concerns freely. They offer empathy, validation, and active listening, which can be immensely comforting for individuals coping with grief. These professionals provide emotional support and help individuals process their grief in a healthy and constructive manner.

Guidance and Coping Strategies

Professional counselors and therapists guide individuals in developing effective coping strategies tailored to their unique needs. They may introduce techniques such as cognitive-behavioral therapy (CBT), mindfulness-based approaches, or grief-specific interventions to help individuals manage their emotions, thoughts, and behaviors. These strategies can empower individuals to navigate their grief and find a path toward healing.

Facilitating Meaning-Making

Grief often involves searching for meaning and making sense of the loss. Professional counselors and therapists can assist individuals in exploring and reconstructing their worldview, identity, and beliefs in the aftermath of loss. They provide support in finding ways to honor the memory of the deceased and integrate the loss into a new narrative of life.

Finding Appropriate Professional Help within The Safe Room

The Safe Room Referral Network

The Safe Room community has established a referral network of trusted professionals specializing in grief counseling and therapy. This network includes licensed counselors, therapists, and psychologists who have expertise in supporting individuals through the grief process. Community members can access this network to find professionals who align with their specific needs and preferences.

Community Recommendations and Testimonials

Within The Safe Room community, individuals can seek recommendations and testimonials from other members who have sought professional help. Sharing personal experiences and insights can help individuals make informed decisions about which professionals may be the best fit for their unique circumstances. Community testimonials provide a sense of trust and reassurance when seeking professional support.

The Safe Room Resource Directory

The Safe Room community maintains a comprehensive resource directory, which includes a list of grief counseling centers, therapists, and other mental health professionals. This directory provides individuals with a curated list of reputable resources and professionals who have experience working with grief-related issues. Community members can explore the directory to find appropriate professional help.

Online Counseling and Teletherapy

The Safe Room community recognizes the importance of

accessibility and offers online counseling and teletherapy options. These services enable individuals to connect with professional counselors and therapists remotely, providing flexibility and convenience. Online counseling platforms within The Safe Room maintain the same level of confidentiality and professionalism as in-person sessions.

Conclusion:

Professional help plays a vital role in supporting individuals through their grief and emotional distress. Professional counselors and therapists bring expertise, emotional support, guidance, and coping strategies to the healing journey. Within The Safe Room community, individuals can access a referral network, seek recommendations, and explore the resource directory to find appropriate professional help. The community also offers online counseling and teletherapy services to ensure accessibility. By embracing the support of professional help within The Safe Room, individuals can find the guidance and tools they need to navigate their grief, heal, and ultimately find hope and meaning in their lives once again.

In the labyrinth of grief, the compassionate guidance of professional counselors and therapists becomes a beacon of light, offering individuals a structured and supportive path on their healing journey. Chapter 12 of "The Safe Room" explores the pivotal role of Seeking Professional Help, providing insights into the benefits of therapeutic intervention and guidance on accessing appropriate resources within The Safe Room.

The Role of Professional Counselors and Therapists in Healing
Grief, with its intricate emotions and complexities, often necessitates the expertise of professionals trained in guiding individuals through the healing process. Professional counselors and therapists within The Safe Room play a crucial role in providing tailored support, offering a safe space for expression, and facilitating the navigation of grief's challenging terrain.

Benefits of Seeking Professional Help:

1. Specialized Expertise:
   - Professional counselors and therapists possess specialized training in grief and trauma.
   - Their expertise allows them to understand the intricacies of grief and provide targeted interventions for healing.

2. Structured Support:
   - Therapy offers a structured and safe environment for individuals to explore and express their emotions.
   - The therapeutic process provides a framework for addressing grief-related challenges in a guided and supportive manner.

3. Validation and Empathy:
   - Professional counselors offer validation and empathy, acknowledging the unique experiences of individuals in their grief

journey.

- The therapeutic relationship becomes a source of understanding and compassion.

4. Coping Skill Development:

- Therapists assist individuals in developing coping skills tailored to their specific needs.

- These skills empower individuals to navigate grief-related stressors and build resilience.

5. Safe Space for Expression:

- Therapy provides a confidential and non-judgmental space for individuals to express their deepest emotions.

- This safe space encourages openness and authenticity in addressing the challenges of grief.

6. Grief Education:

- Counselors provide education on the nature of grief, helping individuals understand the complexities and variations of their emotions.

- Gaining knowledge about grief fosters a sense of empowerment and self-awareness.

Guidance on Finding Appropriate Professional Help Within The Safe Room:

1. Professional Directory:

- Establish a professional directory within The Safe Room,

featuring licensed counselors and therapists specializing in grief support.

- Participants can access this directory to find professionals with expertise in their specific areas of need.

2. Online Counseling Platforms:

- Collaborate with reputable online counseling platforms that offer virtual sessions with licensed therapists.

- Provide information and access to these platforms within The Safe Room, offering individuals the flexibility to receive support remotely.

3. Community Recommendations:

- Facilitate a system for community recommendations within The Safe Room.

- Participants who have had positive experiences with specific therapists can share their recommendations, creating a peer-reviewed resource.

4. Educational Workshops:

- Host educational workshops within The Safe Room, featuring professionals discussing the benefits of therapy and how to find the right therapist.

- These workshops can address common concerns and misconceptions about seeking professional help.

5. Moderator Support:

- Train moderators within The Safe Room to provide guidance

on seeking professional help.

- Moderators can offer information on the importance of therapy, address common questions, and guide individuals in finding suitable resources.

Empowering Through Professional Support: A Collaborative Journey

Chapter 12 recognizes that seeking professional help is a courageous step on the path to healing. Within The Safe Room, individuals are empowered to explore the therapeutic landscape, guided by a community that values the importance of professional intervention. This chapter invites participants to embrace the support of counselors and therapists, recognizing that their expertise serves as a compass, guiding individuals through the complexities of grief toward a place of understanding, resilience, and eventual renewal.

CHAPTER 13

HONORING LOVED ONES

Honoring and remembering loved ones who have passed away is a deeply personal and meaningful practice. This chapter explores various ways to honor the memory of departed loved ones and shares personal stories of remembrance and rituals within The Safe Room community.

Ways to Honor and Remember Loved Ones

1.Creating Memory Keepsakes

Creating memory keepsakes allows individuals to preserve the memory of their loved ones in tangible and meaningful ways. This can include making photo albums or collages, crafting memorial jewelry, or creating a memory box filled with cherished mementos. These keepsakes serve as reminders of the special moments and relationships shared with the departed loved ones.

2. Establishing Rituals and Traditions

Establishing rituals and traditions provides a sense of continuity and connection with loved ones who have passed away. This can involve lighting a candle on special occasions, visiting the grave or a memorial site, or setting aside a specific day each year to celebrate the life and legacy of the departed. Rituals and traditions offer comfort, solace, and an opportunity to reflect on the impact of the loved one's presence in their lives.

3. Volunteering and Charitable Contributions

Engaging in acts of service or making charitable contributions in the name of a loved one can be a powerful way to honor their memory. This can involve volunteering at a cause or organization that was important to the departed, donating to a charitable foundation, or organizing fundraising events in their honor. By giving back to the community in their loved one's name, individuals can continue their legacy of kindness and compassion.

4.Sharing Stories and Memories

Sharing stories and memories is a beautiful way to keep the spirit of departed loved ones alive. Within The Safe Room community, individuals can share anecdotes, photos, or videos of their loved ones, allowing others to connect and remember. This sharing of memories fosters a sense of community, support, and understanding among those who have experienced similar losses.

Personal Stories of Remembrance and Rituals in The Safe Room

Story of Sarah's Garden

Sarah, a member of The Safe Room community, found solace in creating a memorial garden in her backyard. She planted her loved one's favorite flowers and adorned the space with personalized memorial plaques. Sarah spends time in the garden, tending to the plants and reflecting on the cherished memories she shared with her departed loved one.

The Annual Lantern Lighting Ceremony
Every year, The Safe Room community organizes a lantern lighting ceremony to honor departed loved ones. Members gather in a park, each holding a lantern inscribed with the name or message of their loved one. As dusk falls, the lanterns are lit, and they release them into the night sky, symbolizing the love and light that continue to shine in their hearts.

The Memory Quilt Project
Within The Safe Room community, a group of members embarked on a collaborative project to create a memory quilt. Each member contributed a fabric square adorned with a meaningful image or message representing their loved one. The squares were then stitched together to form a quilt that serves as a collective symbol of love, remembrance, and shared experiences.

Conclusion:
Honoring loved ones who have passed away is a deeply personal and significant practice. By creating memory keepsakes, establishing rituals and traditions, engaging in acts of service, and sharing stories and memories, individuals can find comfort, connection, and a sense of continued presence. The Safe Room community provides a supportive space where personal stories of remembrance and rituals are shared, fostering a sense of community

and understanding. Through these practices, individuals within The Safe Room honor the memory of their loved ones and find meaning in their grief journey.

Within the sacred space of grief, Chapter 13 of "The Safe Room" invites individuals to embark on a journey of Honoring Loved Ones—a poignant exploration of ways to commemorate and celebrate the lives of those who have passed away. Here, we weave together stories of remembrance and the diverse tapestry of rituals within The Safe Room community.

Exploring Ways to Honor and Remember:

1. Memorial Tributes:

- Create virtual memorial tributes within The Safe Room, allowing participants to share stories, photographs, and cherished memories of their loved ones.

- These tributes serve as collective expressions of love and remembrance, fostering a sense of shared celebration.

2. Anniversary Commemorations:

- Encourage participants to mark significant anniversaries with meaningful commemorations.

- Whether through virtual events, shared rituals, or personal reflections, these commemorations become a time to honor the enduring impact of those who are dearly missed.

3. Legacy Projects:

- Initiate community projects that celebrate the legacies of departed loved ones.

- Participants can contribute to collaborative endeavors, such as digital scrapbooks, videos, or art installations, capturing the essence of the lives they wish to honor.

4. Acts of Service in Their Memory:
- Inspire individuals to perform acts of service or kindness in memory of their loved ones.
- Whether volunteering, supporting charitable causes, or initiating community projects, these actions become tributes that echo the values and spirit of those who have passed.

5. Symbolic Commemorations:
- Explore the power of symbolism in honoring loved ones.
- Participants can adopt symbolic gestures, such as planting memorial trees, releasing balloons, or creating personalized symbols that hold special significance.

Personal Stories of Remembrance Within The Safe Room:

1. The Annual Virtual Candle Lighting Ceremony:
- Every year, participants come together for a virtual candle lighting ceremony within The Safe Room.
- Each person lights a candle in memory of their loved one, creating a collective glow that symbolizes the enduring presence of those who have passed.

2. Shared Recipes and Favorite Foods:

- Members of The Safe Room community share stories of creating and enjoying their loved ones' favorite recipes.

- This culinary connection becomes a tangible and sensory way to honor the memory of those who delighted in the simple joys of a shared meal.

3. Digital Memory Quilt Project:

- The Safe Room initiated a digital memory quilt project where participants contribute images, stories, and artifacts that represent their loved ones.

- The evolving digital quilt serves as a dynamic and ever-growing mosaic of remembrance within the community.

4. Letters to Heaven:

- A tradition within The Safe Room involves writing letters to loved ones who have passed away.

- Participants express their thoughts, feelings, and updates, fostering a sense of ongoing connection and communication with those they hold dear.

5. Seasonal Memorial Gardens:

- The Safe Room hosts virtual seasonal memorial gardens, providing a changing landscape for participants to contribute symbols and memories.

- Each season brings new additions, creating a living tribute that mirrors the changing seasons of grief.

Benefits of Honoring Loved Ones Within The Safe Room:

1. Fostering Connection:

- Honoring loved ones within The Safe Room fosters a deep sense of connection among participants.

- Shared rituals and commemorations create bonds, reminding individuals that they are not alone in their remembrance.

2. Preserving Legacies:

- The act of honoring loved ones preserves their legacies within the community.

- Through stories, tributes, and symbolic gestures, individuals ensure that the memories of their loved ones endure and inspire.

3. Creating a Culture of Celebration:

- Honoring loved ones transforms grief into a celebration of the lives lived.

- The Safe Room becomes a space where participants share in the joyous memories, laughter, and unique qualities of those they hold close to their hearts.

4. Providing Comfort Through Rituals:

- Rituals of remembrance within The Safe Room provide comfort and solace.

- These rituals become touchstones, offering moments of reflection, connection, and the reassurance that the impact of loved ones endures.

In Honoring, Love Echoes Beyond Goodbye:
Chapter 13 embraces the myriad ways individuals within The Safe

Room choose to honor and remember their loved ones. Through shared stories, rituals, and a collective celebration of legacies, participants discover that even in the face of loss, the love and memories of those who have passed away continue to echo beyond the boundaries of goodbye.

CHAPTER 14

OVERCOMING GUILT AND REGRET

Guilt and regret are common and complex emotions experienced during the grieving process. This chapter addresses the feelings of guilt and regret often associated with loss and provides strategies for processing and releasing these emotions within The Safe Room community.

Understanding Guilt and Regret

1.Guilt: Guilt is the feeling of responsibility or remorse for something one believes they did or failed to do. It may arise from a sense of unfinished business, unresolved conflicts, or perceived shortcomings in the relationship with the departed loved one.

2. Regret: Regret involves feeling sorrow or disappointment about missed opportunities, unfulfilled expectations, or actions taken or not taken in the past. It can stem from wishing for a chance to

make amends or change the course of events.

Strategies for Processing and Releasing Guilt and Regret

1. Self-Compassion and Forgiveness

Practicing self-compassion is crucial when dealing with guilt and regret. Remember that everyone makes mistakes, and it is important to be kind and understanding with yourself. Acknowledge your feelings and thoughts without judgment. Seek forgiveness from yourself and recognize that it is natural to have regrets or guilt in the grieving process.

Open Communication

Within The Safe Room community, open communication plays a vital role in processing guilt and regret. Share your feelings and thoughts with others who have experienced similar emotions. Engage in supportive conversations that validate your experiences and provide different perspectives. The community can offer understanding and empathy, helping you gain insights and acceptance.

Writing and Journaling

Writing and journaling provide a cathartic outlet for processing guilt and regret. Expressing your emotions on paper allows you to reflect, gain clarity, and release pent-up feelings. Within The Safe Room, you can share your writing with the community, fostering a sense of connection and receiving support from others who have gone through similar experiences.

Honoring and Reparation

Taking proactive steps to honor the memory of the departed loved one can be a powerful way to address feelings of guilt and regret. Consider engaging in activities that align with their values or passions. This can include acts of kindness, charitable contributions, or dedicating time to a cause they cared about. By making amends or finding ways to honor their memory, you can find a sense of peace and closure.

Professional Guidance

Seeking professional help within The Safe Room community can provide valuable support in processing guilt and regret. Professional counselors and therapists can offer guidance tailored to your specific circumstances, helping you navigate these complex emotions and develop coping strategies. They can help you reframe your experiences and find ways to move forward with self-compassion and acceptance.

Conclusion:

Guilt and regret are powerful emotions that often accompany grief. Understanding these emotions and applying strategies to process and release them are vital for healing within The Safe Room community. By practicing self-compassion, engaging in open communication, utilizing writing and journaling, finding ways to honor the memory of departed loved ones, and seeking professional guidance when needed, individuals can gradually overcome guilt and regret.

Remember, healing takes time, and by sharing your journey with the supportive community in The Safe Room, you can find solace, understanding, and strength to move forward on your path toward healing.

Guilt and regret, like shadows in the landscape of grief, can cast a heavy burden on the hearts of those mourning a loss. In Chapter 14 of "The Safe Room," we delve into the delicate terrain of Overcoming Guilt and Regret, offering a compassionate exploration of these emotions and providing strategies within The Safe Room to process, release, and find healing.

Understanding Guilt and Regret in Grief:

1. Guilt:

- Guilt often arises from the perception of having failed the departed or from unspoken words and unresolved conflicts.

- Individuals may grapple with the "what-ifs" and engage in self-blame, adding an extra layer of pain to their grief.

2. Regret:

- Regret stems from missed opportunities, unfulfilled intentions, or actions left undone.

- The "could-haves" and "should-haves" may haunt individuals, intensifying the sense of loss and the yearning for a different outcome.

Strategies for Processing and Releasing Guilt and Regret Within The Safe Room:

1. Reflective Writing Sessions:

- Initiate guided reflective writing sessions within The Safe Room, encouraging individuals to explore and articulate their feelings of guilt and regret.

- Writing provides a therapeutic outlet, allowing participants to externalize their emotions and gain clarity on the source of their distress.

2. Supportive Peer Discussions:

- Facilitate peer discussions focused on guilt and regret, creating a safe space within The Safe Room for individuals to share their experiences.

- Peer support can offer insights, empathy, and a sense of communal understanding, reassuring individuals that they are not alone in their struggles.

3. Professional Counseling Sessions:

- Emphasize the importance of seeking professional counseling within The Safe Room to address complex feelings of guilt and regret.

- Trained counselors can guide individuals in navigating these emotions, offering tailored strategies for coping and healing.

4. Guilt and Regret Coping Workshops:

- Organize workshops dedicated to coping with guilt and regret, providing participants with practical tools and coping strategies.

- These workshops can include mindfulness exercises, cognitive-behavioral techniques, and guided self-reflection to help individuals reframe their perspectives.

5. Interactive Art Therapy:

- Introduce interactive art therapy sessions within The Safe Room as a creative outlet for processing guilt and regret.

- Participants can express their emotions through art, allowing for non-verbal exploration and the release of pent-up feelings.

6. Rituals of Forgiveness:

- Create virtual rituals within The Safe Room centered around forgiveness.

- These rituals can include symbolic acts of forgiveness, both for oneself and for the departed, fostering a sense of emotional release and closure.

Embracing Self-Compassion:

1. Self-Compassion Exercises:

- Share self-compassion exercises within The Safe Room, guiding individuals to treat themselves with kindness and understanding.

- Participants can practice self-compassion through affirmations, self-care rituals, and acknowledging their humanity in the face of complex emotions.

2. Mindfulness and Acceptance:

- Introduce mindfulness practices that focus on acceptance and being present in the moment.

- Mindfulness can help individuals let go of the past, fostering a sense of acceptance and peace amid the turmoil of guilt and regret.

3. Community Forgiveness Ceremonies:

- Facilitate community forgiveness ceremonies within The Safe Room, where participants collectively engage in forgiveness rituals.

- These ceremonies create a sense of communal support, reinforcing the idea that forgiveness is a shared journey.

4. Cultivating Gratitude:

- Encourage the practice of cultivating gratitude as a counterbalance to guilt and regret.

- Participants can create gratitude journals or engage in discussions within The Safe Room that focus on the positive aspects of their relationships with their departed loved ones.

In The Safe Room, Compassion Prevails:

Chapter 14 within The Safe Room extends an empathetic hand to those grappling with guilt and regret, recognizing these emotions as integral parts of the grief journey. By fostering an environment of understanding, peer support, and professional guidance, individuals are gently guided towards the path of self-compassion and healing. In The Safe Room, the collective warmth of shared experiences becomes a powerful force, affirming that in the face of guilt and regret, compassion prevails.

CHAPTER 15

FINDING MEANING AND PURPOSE

Finding meaning and purpose in the midst of grief is a transformative and healing process. This chapter delves into the search for meaning and purpose during times of loss and explores how individuals can discover new meaning and purpose within The

Safe Room community.

The Search for Meaning and Purpose

The Impact of Loss

Experiencing loss can deeply challenge our sense of meaning and purpose in life. It can raise existential questions and lead to a reevaluation of our values, beliefs, and priorities. The search for meaning and purpose becomes an essential part of the healing journey, as it helps individuals find new ways to navigate life after loss.

Reflection and Self-Exploration

Grief provides an opportunity for deep reflection and self-exploration. By examining their values, passions, and aspirations, individuals can gain insights into what truly matters to them. They may discover new interests, strengths, or desires that can shape their path toward finding meaning and purpose.

Connecting with the Deceased

Finding meaning and purpose can also involve finding ways to maintain a connection with the departed loved one. This may include carrying on their legacy, honoring their values, or engaging in activities that were important to them. By keeping their memory alive, individuals can find solace and a sense of continuity in their own lives.

Finding Meaning and Purpose within The Safe Room

Community

Sharing Experiences and Insights

Within The Safe Room community, individuals can share their experiences and insights related to finding meaning and purpose after loss. By engaging in conversations and listening to others' stories, members can gain inspiration, different perspectives, and a sense of belonging. Sharing personal journeys can help individuals make meaning of their own experiences and find purpose in supporting others.

Collaborative Projects and Initiatives

The Safe Room community provides opportunities for members to participate in collaborative projects and initiatives. These endeavors can be centered around spreading awareness about grief and loss, supporting charitable causes, or creating platforms for sharing stories of resilience and hope. Through these collective efforts, individuals can find a renewed sense of purpose and contribute to a greater cause.

Mentoring and Support

Within The Safe Room, individuals can also find mentoring and support from others who have walked a similar path. Mentors can provide guidance, wisdom, and encouragement as individuals navigate their search for meaning and purpose. They can offer insights based on their own experiences, helping others discover new possibilities and perspectives.

Self-Exploration Activities and Workshops

The Safe Room community offers self-exploration activities and workshops designed to help individuals explore their passions, values, and aspirations. These resources can guide members in uncovering their unique strengths and interests, leading them to discover new avenues for meaning and purpose. Engaging in these activities within a supportive community fosters a sense of connection and shared growth.

Conclusion:

Finding meaning and purpose in the aftermath of loss is a deeply personal and transformative journey. The Safe Room community provides a nurturing environment where individuals can explore this search together. By sharing experiences, engaging in collaborative projects, accessing mentoring and support, and participating in self-exploration activities, individuals can discover new sources of meaning and purpose. Within The Safe Room, the collective wisdom and support of the community empower individuals to navigate their grief and find a renewed sense of hope, resilience, and purpose in their lives.

Grief, with its profound and transformative nature, often propels individuals on a quest for meaning and purpose amid the shadows of loss. Chapter 15 of "The Safe Room" embarks on a journey of introspection, exploring the profound search for Finding Meaning and Purpose within the intricate tapestry of grief. Here, we delve into how individuals can discover new avenues of significance and purpose within the supportive embrace of The Safe Room community.

The Quest for Meaning Amid Grief:

1. Existential Reflection:

- Grief often prompts existential questioning, compelling individuals to seek deeper meanings in the face of profound loss.

- Questions of purpose, life's significance, and the enduring impact of the departed become central to the grief journey.

2. Reframing Perspectives:

- Individuals may undergo a process of reframing their perspectives on life, relationships, and personal goals.

- Grief can catalyze a reassessment of values, priorities, and the pursuit of a life that aligns with newfound insights.

Discovering Meaning and Purpose Within The Safe Room:

1. Shared Wisdom and Stories:

- Foster a space within The Safe Room for individuals to share their personal journeys of finding meaning amid grief.

- Personal stories become beacons of inspiration, offering insights into how others have navigated the search for purpose.

2. Virtual Workshops on Meaning-Making:

- Organize virtual workshops within The Safe Room focused on meaning-making during grief.

- Trained facilitators can guide participants through exercises and discussions that illuminate pathways to discovering purpose.

3. Collaborative Projects:

- Initiate collaborative projects within The Safe Room that contribute to a sense of collective purpose.

- Participants can engage in projects that support charitable causes, community initiatives, or creative endeavors, fostering a shared sense of impact.

4. Legacy Building Activities:

- Encourage activities that contribute to building legacies within The Safe Room.

- Whether through digital archives, memorial projects, or creative expressions, individuals can participate in activities that leave lasting imprints, creating a sense of ongoing purpose.

Community Support in the Search for Meaning:

1. Empathy and Understanding:

- Cultivate an environment within The Safe Room where empathy and understanding prevail.

- Participants can share their struggles and triumphs in the search for meaning, finding solace in the shared experiences of others.

2. Peer Mentoring Programs:

- Establish peer mentoring programs within The Safe Room.

- Individuals who have found meaning and purpose amid grief

can serve as mentors, offering guidance and support to those currently navigating this transformative journey.

3. Resource Hub for Purposeful Living:

- Curate a resource hub within The Safe Room that provides information on purposeful living, post-grief.

- Articles, videos, and expert insights can guide individuals in exploring different avenues of meaning and purpose.

Inspirational Narratives Within The Safe Room:

1. Rediscovering Passion:

- Within The Safe Room, participants share narratives of rediscovering or uncovering new passions and interests.

- These stories inspire others to explore their own interests as a means of infusing life with purpose.

2. Community Impact Initiatives:

- Celebrate stories of individuals within The Safe Room who have channeled grief into community impact initiatives.

- Whether through advocacy, volunteerism, or creative expression, these narratives exemplify the transformative power of purposeful living.

3. Connecting Through Shared Values:

- The Safe Room becomes a space where individuals connect over shared values and purposes.

- Collaborative endeavors and discussions within the

community contribute to a sense of belonging and shared purpose.

Navigating the Landscape of Meaning:

Chapter 15 unfolds as a guide through the intricate landscape of meaning-making in grief. Within The Safe Room, individuals are encouraged to explore, question, and connect with a community that understands the depths of their search. This chapter illuminates paths of renewal, reminding participants that even in the midst of grief, the quest for meaning and purpose becomes a powerful catalyst for transformation and healing.

.

CHAPTER 16

RESILIENCE AND GROWTH

Resilience plays a vital role in the healing process after experiencing grief and loss. This chapter explores the concept of resilience and its significance in navigating the challenges of loss. Additionally, it shares stories of resilience and growth within The Safe Room community, showcasing the transformative power of resilience in the face of adversity.

Understanding Resilience: The Definition of Resilience
Resilience refers to the ability to bounce back, adapt, and thrive in the face of adversity or challenging circumstances. It involves harnessing inner strengths, coping skills, and support systems to navigate difficult emotions and situations.

Resilience and Grief
In the context of grief, resilience is the capacity to heal, grow, and find meaning in the midst of loss. It does not mean avoiding or suppressing emotions but rather embracing them as part of the healing journey. Resilience enables individuals to integrate their loss into their lives and move forward with renewed hope and strength.

Stories of Resilience and Growth within The Safe Room

Sarah's Journey Towards Healing
Sarah, a member of The Safe Room community, experienced the sudden loss of her spouse. Initially overwhelmed by grief, she found solace and support within the community. Through counseling and the shared experiences of other members, Sarah learned coping strategies and gradually embraced her resilience. She began volunteering at a grief support center, helping others navigate their grief. Sarah's journey exemplifies how resilience can lead to personal growth and the ability to support others on their healing path.

Mark's Transformative Loss

Mark, a member of The Safe Room, lost his sibling to a tragic accident. Initially consumed by grief and guilt, he struggled to find meaning in the loss. Through engaging in open discussions and receiving support from the community, Mark discovered his resilience and began to honor his sibling's memory by raising awareness about the importance of mental health. Mark's journey showcases how resilience can lead to personal growth and the creation of a meaningful legacy.

Emma's Path to Self-Rediscovery

Emma, a member of The Safe Room community, faced the loss of her job and the subsequent loss of her identity and purpose. Within the community, Emma explored her passions, engaged in self-reflection, and received support from fellow members. With their encouragement, she pursued a new career aligned with her true calling. Emma's story demonstrates how resilience can lead to personal growth, self-discovery, and the rebuilding of a fulfilling life after loss.

Fostering Resilience within The Safe Room Community

Supportive Network

The Safe Room community serves as a supportive network where individuals can find understanding, empathy, and encouragement. Through shared experiences and conversations, community members provide validation, guidance, and a sense of belonging, fostering resilience in each other.

Resources and Tools

The Safe Room offers various resources and tools designed to help individuals develop and strengthen their resilience. These include workshops, guided meditations, self-care practices, and resilience-building exercises. By engaging with these resources, community members can cultivate their inner strengths and coping mechanisms.

Mentoring and Role Models

Within The Safe Room, individuals can find mentors and role models who have demonstrated resilience in their own journeys. These mentors serve as sources of inspiration, providing guidance and support to those who are navigating their own healing process. The mentorship within the community nurtures resilience and fosters growth.

Conclusion:

Resilience plays a pivotal role in the healing process after experiencing loss. The Safe Room community provides a nurturing environment where individuals can cultivate their resilience and find support as they navigate grief and loss. Through shared experiences, resources, mentoring, and the transformative power of resilience, community members discover their inner strength and capacity for growth. The stories of resilience and growth within The Safe Room illustrate the profound impact resilience can have on personal healing, creating meaning, and finding a renewed sense of purpose in life after loss.

Resilience, an indomitable force woven into the fabric of the human spirit, becomes a guiding light within the profound journey of grief. Chapter 16 of "The Safe Room" explores the transformative power of Resilience and Growth, illuminating the ways in which individuals navigate the challenging terrain of loss and emerge stronger within the supportive embrace of The Safe Room community.

The Essence of Resilience in Grief:

1. Adaptability in Adversity:

   - Resilience is the capacity to adapt and bounce back from adversity.

   - In the context of grief, resilience becomes a dynamic force, enabling individuals to navigate the ever-changing landscape of emotions and challenges.

   2. Strength in Vulnerability:

   - Resilience does not negate vulnerability but exists alongside it.

   - It is the ability to acknowledge pain, face adversity, and find strength in vulnerability that characterizes the resilient spirit.

Stories of Resilience Within The Safe Room:

   1. From Grief to Advocacy:

   - Members of The Safe Room community share stories of

transforming personal grief into advocacy.

- Individuals channel their pain into initiatives that raise awareness, support others, and effect positive change within the broader community.

2. Finding Purpose in Creativity:

- Creative expressions become avenues for resilience and growth within The Safe Room.

- Participants share stories of discovering newfound purpose and strength through artistic endeavors, from painting and writing to music and performance.

3. Navigating Personal Growth Through Loss:

- Personal growth narratives within The Safe Room reveal the profound ways individuals have evolved through the crucible of grief.

- From deepened empathy to increased self-awareness, these stories underscore the potential for growth within the grieving process.

4. Building Bridges of Connection:

- The Safe Room becomes a bridge connecting individuals with shared experiences of loss.

- Stories of resilience highlight the ways in which participants reach out, support one another, and form connections that become integral to their healing.

Facilitating Resilience Within The Safe Room:

1. Resilience-Building Workshops:

- Host virtual workshops within The Safe Room focused on building resilience.

- Trained facilitators guide participants through exercises and discussions aimed at enhancing coping mechanisms and fostering a resilient mindset.

2. Mentorship Programs:

- Establish mentorship programs within The Safe Room where resilient individuals serve as mentors to those navigating early stages of grief.

- Mentorship fosters a sense of guidance, encouragement, and the sharing of practical strategies for building resilience.

3. Interactive Support Groups:

- Create interactive support groups within The Safe Room that focus specifically on resilience and growth.

- Participants can share strategies, challenges, and triumphs, fostering a community of individuals committed to cultivating resilience.

4. Resilience Resource Center:

- Develop a resource center within The Safe Room dedicated to resilience.

- Curate articles, videos, and expert insights on resilience-building techniques, offering participants a wealth of information to support their journey.

In the Soil of Grief, Seeds of Resilience Bloom:

Chapter 16 of "The Safe Room" unfolds as a testament to the remarkable resilience inherent within individuals navigating grief. Within the nourishing soil of shared experiences and empathetic community, the seeds of resilience take root and bloom. Through stories of growth, strength, and the indomitable human spirit, this chapter illuminates the transformative journey that unfolds within The Safe Room, where resilience becomes a beacon of hope amid the shadows of loss.

CHAPTER 17

SUPPORTING OTHERS

Supporting others who are grieving is a vital aspect of The Safe Room community. This chapter offers guidance on how to provide support within the community and emphasizes the importance of empathy, active listening, and offering comfort to those in need.

The Role of Support in Grief

Support plays a crucial role in the healing journey of individuals who are grieving. It provides a safe space for expression, validation, and connection. By offering support, community members can help alleviate feelings of isolation and contribute to the overall well-being of those in need.

The Importance of Empathy

Empathy is the ability to understand and share the feelings of another person. It is a key component of effective support. Empathy allows community members to connect with and validate the experiences of those who are grieving, fostering a sense of understanding and compassion.

Supporting Others Within The Safe Room

Active Listening

Active listening is an essential skill when supporting others within The Safe Room community. It involves fully focusing on the speaker, suspending judgment, and providing a non-judgmental space for them to express their thoughts and emotions. Practice active listening by maintaining eye contact, nodding, and providing verbal and non-verbal cues that show you are fully engaged in the conversation.

Validation and Empathy

Validate the emotions and experiences of others by acknowledging their pain and offering empathy. Let them know that their feelings are valid and understandable. Use phrases such as, "I can imagine how difficult that must be for you" or "Your feelings are completely valid, and I'm here to support you." This demonstrates that you are present and willing to listen without judgment.

Offering Comfort

Offering comfort within The Safe Room community can take various forms. It may involve sending virtual hugs, sharing comforting words, or expressing genuine concern and care. Simple gestures like sending supportive messages or checking in on someone can go a long way in providing comfort and reassurance.

Avoiding Comparison and Judgment

When supporting others, it is important to avoid comparing their experiences to your own or making judgments about their grief process. Each person's journey is unique, and it is crucial to respect their individual experiences and emotions. Focus on understanding and validating their feelings rather than imposing your own perspective.

Engaging in Community Support

Participating in Discussions

Engage in discussions within The Safe Room community to offer support. Share your own experiences, insights, and words of encouragement. By actively participating, you contribute to the collective support network and create a sense of solidarity.

Sharing Resources and Information

If you come across helpful resources, articles, or books related to grief and healing, share them within The Safe Room community. These resources can provide valuable information and support to those who are grieving, offering additional tools for their healing journey.

Encouraging Professional Help

While community support is vital, acknowledge that professional help may be necessary for some individuals. Encourage those who are struggling to seek the assistance of therapists, counselors, or grief support groups. Within The Safe Room community, share information about reputable professionals or resources that can provide specialized guidance.

Conclusion:

Supporting others within The Safe Room community is a fundamental aspect of fostering healing and resilience. By practicing empathy, active listening, and offering comfort, community members can create a safe space for individuals to express their grief and find solace. Remember to validate others' experiences, avoid judgment, and encourage professional help when needed. Within the supportive community of The Safe Room, each member has the potential to make a significant difference in the lives of those who are grieving, offering compassion, understanding, and a sense of belonging.

Within the sanctuary of grief that is The Safe Room, Chapter 17 unfolds as a heartfelt guide on Supporting Others, recognizing the profound impact of empathy, active listening, and offering comfort within this empathetic community. In this chapter, we explore the delicate art of being a source of solace for those navigating the intricate pathways of grief.

The Gentle Art of Empathy:

1. Understanding Grief's Landscape:

- Before extending support, cultivate an understanding of the diverse and complex terrain of grief.

- Recognize that grief is a unique journey for each individual, with its own ebbs, flows, and nuances.

2. Empathetic Presence:

- Be present with an empathetic heart, offering a space where individuals can express their feelings without judgment.

- Empathy is the cornerstone of effective support, validating the emotions of the grieving and fostering a sense of connection.

Guidance on Active Listening:

1. Creating a Listening Space:

- Actively listen with an open heart, creating a space where individuals feel heard and understood.

- Avoid interrupting or rushing the process, allowing the speaker to share at their own pace.

2. Reflective Responses:

- Respond reflectively to affirm that you have heard and understood the emotions shared.

- Phrases like "I hear you," or "Your feelings are valid," convey empathy and validation.

3. Avoiding Judgment:

- Suspend judgment and resist the urge to offer unsolicited advice or comparisons.

- Allow the grieving individual to navigate their emotions without feeling pressured to conform to preconceived notions of grief.

The Language of Comfort:

1. Words of Compassion:

- Offer words of compassion that acknowledge the depth of loss without attempting to minimize or rationalize the pain.

- Simple expressions like "I'm here for you" or "I'm so sorry for your loss" convey heartfelt support.

2. Expressing Comfort Through Actions:

- Sometimes, actions speak louder than words. Offer practical support, such as preparing a meal, running errands, or providing a listening ear.

- Small gestures can have a profound impact, demonstrating that the community within The Safe Room stands as a collective support system.

Building a Supportive Community:

1. Community Guidelines:
   - Establish and communicate clear guidelines within The Safe Room that emphasize a culture of compassion, respect, and support.
   - Encourage members to adhere to these guidelines, creating a safe and nurturing space for all.

2. Community-Led Support Initiatives:
   - Facilitate community-led support initiatives where individuals actively reach out to others in need.
   - This may include virtual support circles, buddy systems, or outreach programs that foster a sense of shared responsibility.

3. Moderator-Mediated Support Channels:
   - Implement support channels moderated by trained individuals within The Safe Room.
   - Moderators can provide additional guidance, resources, and ensure that conversations remain supportive and constructive.

Navigating Difficult Conversations:

1. Sensitive Language Use:
   - Encourage the use of sensitive language within The Safe Room, fostering an environment where individuals feel safe discussing difficult topics.
   - Provide guidance on framing responses with empathy and avoiding language that may inadvertently cause distress.

2. Respecting Boundaries:

- Emphasize the importance of respecting individual boundaries and personal choices in grief.

- Not everyone may be ready to engage in certain conversations, and fostering a culture of respect allows for diverse and personal grief experiences.

The Ripple Effect of Compassion:

Chapter 17 serves as a beacon within The Safe Room, guiding individuals on how to extend a compassionate embrace to those traversing the landscape of grief. Through the language of empathy, the art of active listening, and the warmth of comforting gestures, the community within The Safe Room becomes a testament to the profound impact of shared support. In every act of compassion, a ripple of comfort is born, creating a nurturing environment where grief is met with understanding, and no one walks alone.

CHAPTER 18

DEALING WITH TRIGGERS AND ANNIVERSARIES

Grief is an intricate journey with its share of poignant moments, and Chapter 18 of "The Safe Room" gently explores the terrain of Dealing with Triggers and Anniversaries. Within this chapter, we delve into the challenges posed by common triggers and the emotional weight of significant dates, offering coping strategies and a supportive sanctuary within The Safe Room.

Understanding Triggers and Anniversaries:

1. Common Triggers:

- Triggers are stimuli that evoke strong emotional responses linked to the loss.

- Common triggers include places, objects, anniversaries, or specific activities associated with the departed.

2. Impact of Anniversaries:

- Anniversaries and significant dates magnify the intensity of grief.

- Birthdays, anniversaries of the passing, and other commemorative dates can evoke a range of emotions, from sadness to nostalgia.

Coping Strategies Within The Safe Room:

1. Preparation and Planning:

- Encourage individuals to plan for challenging dates in advance.

- Within The Safe Room, provide resources and discussions on creating self-care plans for anniversaries, offering proactive strategies to navigate the emotional waves.

2. Virtual Commemoration Events:

- Facilitate virtual commemoration events within The Safe Room.

- Participants can collectively honor their loved ones, sharing stories, rituals, or moments of reflection in a supportive community setting.

3. Guided Coping Workshops:

- Conduct guided coping workshops within The Safe Room specifically tailored for triggers and anniversaries.

- Trained facilitators can lead discussions on coping mechanisms, mindfulness practices, and creating personalized rituals for these emotionally charged moments.

4. Supportive Peer Discussions:

- Foster peer discussions within The Safe Room where individuals share their experiences and coping strategies.

- Hearing others' stories can provide a sense of connection and offer diverse perspectives on navigating triggers and anniversaries.

Triggers and anniversaries can bring forth intense emotions and challenges for individuals who are grieving. This chapter explores common triggers and difficulties faced during significant dates and provides coping strategies and support available within The Safe Room community to navigate these times of heightened sensitivity.

Understanding Triggers and Anniversaries

Triggers are stimuli that evoke strong emotional responses and remind individuals of their loss. They can be anything from a specific date, a particular location, or even a song. Triggers have the power to reignite grief and intensify emotions, making it important to recognize and address their impact.

Challenges of Anniversaries and Significant Dates

Anniversaries and significant dates, such as birthdays or holidays, can be particularly challenging for those who are grieving. These occasions often amplify feelings of loss and absence, as they serve as reminders of what once was and what is now changed.

Coping Strategies for Triggers and Anniversaries

Self-Care and Emotional Preparation

Prioritize self-care leading up to triggers and anniversaries. Engage in activities that promote well-being, such as exercise, mindfulness, journaling, or spending time in nature. Additionally, emotionally prepare yourself by acknowledging the potential challenges and allowing space for the emotions that may arise.

Planning and Rituals

Create a plan for significant dates and anniversaries. This may involve developing rituals or traditions that honor and remember the loved one. Engage in activities that hold personal meaning, such as writing a letter, visiting a memorial site, or sharing stories and memories with others.

Seeking Support within The Safe Room

Lean on the support available within The Safe Room community during triggering times. Share your concerns, fears, and emotions with fellow members who understand the complexities of grief. Engage in discussions specifically focused on triggers and anniversaries, as these can provide guidance, insights, and validation.

Professional Assistance

Consider seeking professional assistance from therapists or grief counselors who specialize in helping individuals navigate triggers and significant dates. The Safe Room community can offer recommendations and resources to connect with professionals who understand the unique challenges of grief.

Support Available Within The Safe Room

Trigger Support Groups

The Safe Room offers trigger support groups where individuals with shared experiences can gather to discuss coping strategies, share personal stories, and provide mutual support during triggering times. These groups provide a safe and empathetic space to navigate the challenges of triggers and anniversaries.

Guided Meditations and Mindfulness Practices

Within The Safe Room, you can access guided meditations and mindfulness practices specifically designed to help manage triggers and navigate emotional intensity. These resources can assist in grounding oneself, managing anxiety, and fostering self-compassion during triggering moments.

Virtual Gatherings and Events

The Safe Room community organizes virtual gatherings and events during significant dates and anniversaries. These gatherings offer a supportive environment for individuals to come together, share their stories, and find solace in the collective strength of the community.

Building a Supportive Environment:

1. Community Sensitivity Campaigns:

- Launch community sensitivity campaigns within The Safe Room to raise awareness about triggers and anniversaries.

- Through informational posts and discussions, create an environment that fosters empathy and understanding during these challenging times.

2. Moderator-Led Support Circles:

- Have moderators lead special support circles within The Safe Room during peak triggering periods.

- Moderators can provide additional guidance, resources, and a comforting presence to those seeking support.

3. Resource Hub for Coping:

- Curate a resource hub within The Safe Room that focuses on coping strategies for triggers and anniversaries.

- Provide articles, videos, and expert insights to equip individuals with a toolbox of coping mechanisms.

Encouraging Personal Reflection:

1. Digital Journaling:

- Promote digital journaling within The Safe Room as a means of personal reflection.

- Participants can express their emotions, document their coping strategies, and track their personal growth through these challenging moments.

2. Artistic Expression:

- Encourage artistic expression within The Safe Room during triggering periods.

- Whether through writing, visual arts, or music, participants can channel their emotions into creative outlets that become both cathartic and empowering.

Guidance for Supporting Others:

1. Empathetic Messaging:

- Guide members of The Safe Room on crafting empathetic

messages to support others during triggering events.

- Encourage expressions of empathy, understanding, and offers of virtual companionship.

2. Virtual Buddy System:

- Implement a virtual buddy system within The Safe Room where members can connect with someone for mutual support during triggering periods.

- Having a virtual buddy provides an additional layer of companionship and understanding.

In the Shelter of The Safe Room:
Conclusion:

Triggers and anniversaries can be emotionally challenging for individuals who are grieving. By employing coping strategies such as self-care, planning, seeking support, and engaging in professional assistance, individuals can navigate these times with greater resilience. Within The Safe Room community, members can find understanding, support, and resources specifically tailored to managing triggers and anniversaries. By leaning on the collective wisdom and empathy of the community, individuals can find comfort, validation, and strength as they navigate these sensitive moments of remembrance and grief.

Chapter 18 within The Safe Room extends a compassionate hand to guide individuals through the sensitive milestones of triggers and anniversaries. As the community collectively acknowledges the weight of these moments, The Safe Room becomes a shelter of understanding, offering solace, resources, and the comforting presence of shared experiences. In every shared reflection, coping strategy, and empathetic exchange, The Safe Room stands as a sanctuary where the challenges of triggers and anniversaries are met with unity, compassion, and unwavering support.

CHAPTER 19

PARENTING THROUGH GRIEF

Parenting while grieving presents unique challenges and complexities. This chapter addresses the difficulties faced by parents who are navigating grief and provides support and resources available within The Safe Room community to help them on this journey.

Balancing Personal Grief and Parenting Responsibilities

Parenting through grief requires finding a delicate balance between attending to one's own emotional needs and fulfilling the responsibilities of parenting. It can be challenging to manage personal grief while also providing emotional support and stability for children.

Parenting through grief is a challenging and emotional journey. When a parent is grieving, they not only have to navigate their own grief but also provide support and care for their children. Here are some suggestions for parenting through grief:

1. Communicate Openly and Honestly: Be open and honest with your children about the loss and share information that is appropriate for their age and understanding. Use simple and clear language to explain what has happened and answer their questions truthfully. Encourage them to express their feelings and emotions.

2. Create a Safe Space for Expression: Allow your children to express their grief in their own way. Encourage them to talk about their feelings, ask questions, and share memories of the person who has passed away. Be attentive and compassionate listeners, providing validation and support as they navigate their own grief.

3. Maintain Routines and Structure: Children thrive on routines and structure, which can provide a sense of stability and security during times of grief. Try to maintain regular schedules for meals, bedtime, and activities as much as possible. Consistency can help children feel grounded and provide a sense of normalcy during a challenging time.

4. Seek Age-Appropriate Resources: Look for age-appropriate books, videos, or other resources that explain grief and loss to children. These resources can help them understand their emotions and provide guidance on how to cope with their feelings. Utilize resources that address grief in a way that resonates with your child's developmental stage.

5. Encourage Expression through Art and Play: Children often express their emotions through creative outlets such as art, play, or storytelling. Encourage them to engage in activities that allow them to express their grief in a safe and creative manner. Provide art supplies, encourage imaginative play, or create memory boxes together to honor the person who has passed away.

6. Seek Support for Yourself: It's essential to prioritize your own self-care and seek support as a grieving parent. Reach out to friends, family, or support groups for emotional support. Consider speaking with a therapist or counselor who specializes in grief to help you navigate your own grief journey while simultaneously supporting your children.

7. Normalize Grief as a Family: Help your children understand that grief is a natural part of life and that it affects everyone differently. Normalize the range of emotions they may experience and let them know that it is okay to grieve in their own way. Encourage open conversations about grief as a family, fostering an environment where everyone's feelings are acknowledged and respected.

8. Lean on Your Support Network: Reach out to your support network for assistance and guidance. Trusted family members, friends, or professionals can help provide additional support to you and your children. Don't hesitate to ask for help when needed.

Remember, every child is unique, and their grief journey will be individual to them. Adapt your parenting approach based on your child's age, temperament, and understanding. Be patient, loving, and understanding as you navigate your own grief while supporting your children through their grief process.

Modeling Healthy Grief Responses
Parents play a crucial role in modeling healthy grief responses for

their children. It can be overwhelming to manage their own emotions while also guiding their children through the grieving process. Parents may question their ability to provide the necessary support and worry about the impact of their grief on their children.

Support and Resources for Parenting through Grief
The Safe Room Parenting Support Groups

The Safe Room offers dedicated parenting support groups where parents can connect with others who are navigating similar challenges. These groups provide a safe space for sharing experiences, seeking advice, and receiving validation. They offer an opportunity to connect with fellow parents who understand the complexities of parenting through grief.

Coping Strategies for Parents

The Safe Room community provides coping strategies specifically tailored to parents navigating grief. These strategies include self-care practices, setting boundaries, seeking professional help, and finding ways to communicate with children about grief in age-appropriate ways. The community can offer guidance and insights from others who have walked a similar path.

Online Workshops and Webinars

The Safe Room organizes online workshops and webinars that address the unique challenges of parenting through grief. These educational resources provide valuable insights and practical tools for parents to navigate their grief while supporting their children effectively.

Recommendations for Children's Books and Resources

Within The Safe Room community, members can share recommendations for children's books, articles, and resources that help parents explain grief to their children and support their understanding and healing. These resources can assist parents in finding age-appropriate language and activities to facilitate open conversations about grief.

Building a Supportive Network

Connecting with Other Parents

Parents in The Safe Room community can connect with one another to share experiences, exchange advice, and provide support. By forming connections with fellow parents who understand the challenges of parenting through grief, individuals can find comfort, validation, and a sense of community.

Engaging in Family-Focused Discussions

Participating in family-focused discussions within The Safe Room community can provide parents with insights and strategies for navigating grief within the family unit. These discussions can cover topics such as maintaining routines, fostering open communication, and creating meaningful family rituals to honor and remember the loved one.

Seeking Professional Guidance

The Safe Room community can offer recommendations for

therapists, counselors, or grief support professionals who specialize in supporting parents and families through the grieving process. Professional guidance can provide personalized strategies and support tailored to the unique needs of each family.

Conclusion:

Parenting through grief presents unique challenges, but with support and resources, parents can navigate this complex journey. Within The Safe Room community, parents can find solace, understanding, and guidance from others who have experienced similar struggles. By participating in support groups, accessing coping strategies, and connecting with other parents, individuals can find strength, validation, and practical tools to parent effectively while tending to their own grief. Remember, you are not alone in this journey, and The Safe Room community stands ready to support you every step of the way.

Parenting through grief is a profound journey, laden with unique challenges and complexities. In Chapter 19 of "The Safe Room," we delve into the delicate balance of Parenting through Grief, addressing the distinctive challenges faced by parents navigating loss and offering a nurturing space within The Safe Room for guidance, support, and shared understanding.

Navigating the Dual Role:

1. Balancing Emotions:

- Parents often find themselves balancing their own grief while striving to provide emotional support to their children.

- Acknowledge the intricate interplay of emotions, ranging from personal sorrow to the responsibility of fostering a secure environment for the family.

2. Communicating Grief to Children:

- Discuss the importance of age-appropriate conversations about grief with children.

- Within The Safe Room, parents can share experiences, strategies, and resources for effectively communicating the reality of loss to their little ones.

Unique Challenges Faced by Grieving Parents:

1. Guilt and Overwhelm:

- Parents may grapple with guilt over not being able to fully engage or feeling overwhelmed by the dual responsibilities of grief and parenting.

- Provide a space within The Safe Room for parents to express these feelings without judgment, fostering a supportive community.

2. Maintaining Normalcy:

- The challenge of maintaining a sense of normalcy for children while coping with grief is a common struggle.

- Share practical tips and insights within The Safe Room on striking a balance between maintaining routines and allowing space for emotional expression.

Resources and Support for Grieving Parents:

1. Expert-led Parenting Workshops:
- Conduct expert-led parenting workshops within The Safe Room, addressing the unique challenges faced by grieving parents.
- These workshops can provide guidance on age-appropriate conversations, fostering resilience in children, and navigating the evolving dynamics of the family.

2. Peer Support Groups for Parents:
- Establish peer support groups specifically for parents within The Safe Room.
- Parents can share their experiences, exchange advice, and form connections with others who understand the nuances of parenting through grief.

3. Child-Centric Grief Resources:
- Curate a collection of child-centric grief resources within The Safe Room.
- These resources may include books, articles, and activities designed to help parents navigate grief conversations with their children and support their emotional well-being.

Embracing Shared Stories and Strategies:

1. Parenting Narratives within The Safe Room:

- Encourage parents to share their personal narratives within The Safe Room.

- These stories become a source of inspiration, offering insights into diverse parenting approaches, coping mechanisms, and the resilience of families navigating grief.

2. Virtual Playdates and Activities:

- Facilitate virtual playdates and activities within The Safe Room for families.

- Providing a space for parents and children to connect in a lighthearted manner fosters a sense of community and shared experiences beyond grief.

Guiding Parents Toward Professional Support:

1. Navigating Professional Counseling:

- Discuss the role of professional counseling for grieving parents within The Safe Room.

- Provide guidance on finding appropriate counselors or therapists who specialize in supporting families navigating grief.

2. Access to Child-Focused Therapies:

- Highlight resources within The Safe Room that offer child-focused therapeutic support.

- This may include information on play therapy, art therapy, and other approaches designed to help children express and process their emotions.

Fostering Resilience in Children:

1. Empowerment through Open Dialogue:

- Encourage open dialogue within The Safe Room on empowering children through age-appropriate conversations about grief.

- Parents can share their experiences and insights on fostering resilience in children, emphasizing the importance of open communication.

2. Creative Expression for Children:

- Explore creative outlets for children to express their emotions within The Safe Room.

- Parents can share ideas for art, journaling, and other creative activities that provide children with alternative means of expression.

A Haven for Grieving Parents:

Chapter 19 within The Safe Room unfolds as a haven for parents navigating the complex terrain of grief while raising children. It offers a sanctuary where shared stories, resources, and compassionate understanding converge to form a supportive community. In every shared struggle, triumph, and collaborative endeavor, The Safe Room becomes a pillar of strength for parents, guiding them through the nuanced journey of parenting through grief with resilience and unwavering compassion.

CHAPTER 20

CULTIVATING HOPE

Cultivating hope during the grieving process is essential for healing and resilience. In this chapter, we will explore the importance of hope and share stories of hope and resilience found within The Safe Room community.

The Essence of Hope in Grief:

1. A Guiding Light in Darkness:

- Hope serves as a guiding light, offering solace and direction in the darkest moments of grief.

- Explore the ways in which cultivating hope becomes a transformative force, providing individuals with the strength to navigate the complexities of loss.

2. An Anchor in the Storm:

- In the turbulent seas of grief, hope becomes an anchor that grounds individuals and prevents them from being entirely consumed by sorrow.

- Discuss the stabilizing effect of hope, providing a sense of purpose and resilience in the face of adversity.

Stories of Hope Within The Safe Room:

1. Resilience in Shared Narratives:

- Within The Safe Room, members share personal narratives that reflect the resilient spirit's ability to find hope amidst grief.

- These stories serve as beacons, illuminating the transformative journey from despair to the cultivation of hope.

2. Turning Pain into Purpose:

- Explore stories of individuals within The Safe Room who have turned their pain into purpose.

- Witness the powerful narrative of how hope emerges when individuals channel their grief into initiatives that contribute to positive change and support within the community.

3. Community Support as a Source of Hope:

- Share instances within The Safe Room where the community itself becomes a source of hope.

- Stories may revolve around the collective strength found in shared experiences, offering comfort, guidance, and unwavering support.

Cultivating Hope Within The Safe Room:

1. Hope-Centric Workshops:

- Conduct workshops within The Safe Room that focus specifically on cultivating hope.

- Trained facilitators can guide participants through exercises and discussions aimed at nurturing a hopeful mindset in the midst of grief.

2. Hope Journaling:

- Encourage hope journaling within The Safe Room as a daily

practice.

- Participants can reflect on moments of hope, no matter how small, fostering a positive outlook and creating a record of resilience.

3. Virtual Hope Circles:

- Facilitate virtual hope circles within The Safe Room, where individuals share stories and insights on finding hope in unexpected places.

- These circles become a collective wellspring of inspiration and encouragement.

Nurturing Hope Through Connection:

1. Connection as a Catalyst for Hope:

- Explore the role of connection in nurturing hope within The Safe Room.

- Discuss how forming meaningful connections with others on similar journeys becomes a catalyst for cultivating hope.

2. Hope-Focused Resources:

- Curate a collection of hope-focused resources within The Safe Room.

- These resources may include articles, videos, and expert insights on fostering hope, resilience, and a positive mindset during grief.

Hope as a Transformative Force:

1. The Ripple Effect of Hope:

- Illustrate how cultivating hope within The Safe Room creates a ripple effect that extends beyond individual experiences.

- Stories can highlight how one person's journey toward hope inspires and uplifts others within the community.

2. Hope as a Companion on the Journey:

- Emphasize the idea that hope becomes a steadfast companion throughout the grief journey.

- Share stories within The Safe Room that depict how individuals, with hope as their guiding force, navigate the complexities of grief with courage and resilience.

The Importance of Cultivating Hope

Cultivating hope is a powerful and essential practice, especially during challenging times like grief. Here are some ways to cultivate hope:

1. Acknowledge and Accept Grief: It's important to acknowledge and accept your grief as a natural response to loss. Allow yourself to experience and process your emotions without judgment. Recognize that grief is a normal part of life and that it takes time to heal.

2. Set Realistic Expectations: Understand that healing and finding hope take time. Set realistic expectations for yourself and acknowledge that the grieving process is unique to each individual.

Be patient with yourself as you navigate your grief journey.

3. Seek Support: Surround yourself with a supportive network of family, friends, or support groups. Sharing your feelings and experiences with others who have gone through similar challenges can provide comfort, validation, and a sense of hope. Professional counseling or therapy can also be beneficial in navigating grief and fostering hope.

4. Practice Self-Care: Prioritize self-care to nurture your physical, emotional, and mental well-being. Engage in activities that bring you joy, relaxation, and a sense of peace. This can include exercise, spending time in nature, practicing mindfulness or meditation, engaging in hobbies, or seeking creative outlets.

5. Find Meaning and Purpose: Seek ways to find meaning and purpose in your life, even amidst grief. Engage in activities that align with your values and bring fulfillment, such as volunteering, supporting a cause related to your loved one, or helping others who are experiencing similar challenges. Connecting with a sense of purpose can help cultivate hope and resilience.

6. Practice Gratitude: Cultivate a practice of gratitude by focusing on the positive aspects of your life, even in the midst of grief. Take time each day to reflect on the things you are grateful for, whether they are simple or significant. This practice can shift your perspective and foster a sense of hope and appreciation.

7. Embrace Moments of Joy: Allow yourself to experience moments of joy and happiness, even while grieving. It's not about forgetting or minimizing your loss, but rather finding balance and allowing yourself to experience positive emotions. Engage in activities that bring you joy, spend time with loved ones, or create new positive memories.

8. Focus on Personal Growth: Use your grief as an opportunity for personal growth and transformation. Explore ways to develop resilience, strength, and compassion. Engage in self-reflection, seek opportunities for learning and personal development, and focus on building a stronger and more meaningful life.

Remember that cultivating hope is a gradual and ongoing process. It may ebb and flow, and that's okay. Be gentle with yourself as you navigate your grief and focus on nurturing hope within yourself, even in the face of adversity.

Finding Meaning and Purpose

Cultivating hope provides individuals with a sense of meaning and purpose in their grief journey. Hope allows them to envision a future where healing and growth are possible, even in the midst of pain and loss. It motivates individuals to seek healing and find ways to honor their loved ones.

Nurturing Resilience

Hope nourishes resilience, enabling individuals to bounce back from adversity and find strength in the face of challenges. It provides the determination to persevere and the belief that they can overcome the pain of grief and rebuild their lives.

Stories of Hope and Resilience

Sarah's Story: Finding Joy in Memories

Sarah, a member of The Safe Room community, lost her husband unexpectedly. Initially consumed by grief, she found solace within the community. Through sharing her story and connecting with others, Sarah discovered that embracing her memories and finding joy in them brought her comfort and a renewed sense of hope. She now treasures her husband's legacy and has become an advocate for living life fully in honor of those we have lost.

Michael's Story: Transforming Grief into Purpose

Michael's son passed away after a long battle with illness. Devastated by the loss, Michael sought support within The Safe Room. Through conversations with other members, he discovered a deep desire to help other families enduring similar struggles. Michael founded a nonprofit organization that provides support and resources for families with critically ill children. His journey exemplifies how hope can be transformed into purpose, turning personal tragedy into a catalyst for positive change.

Fostering Hope within The Safe Room

Hope-Sharing Discussions

The Safe Room community encourages hope-sharing discussions, where members can exchange stories, experiences, and strategies for fostering hope in the midst of grief. These discussions provide inspiration and serve as reminders that hope can be found even in the darkest moments.

Resilience-Building Resources

The Safe Room offers resilience-building resources, such as articles, podcasts, and workshops, to empower individuals to cultivate hope in their grief journey. These resources provide practical tools, guidance, and insights from experts and those who have experienced similar challenges.

Celebrating Milestones and Victories

Within The Safe Room community, members celebrate milestones and victories, no matter how small, as a way to foster hope and resilience. By acknowledging progress, sharing achievements, and supporting one another, individuals find encouragement and motivation to continue their healing journey.

Conclusion:

Cultivating hope is a vital aspect of the grieving process. It provides meaning, resilience, and the belief that healing and growth are possible. Within The Safe Room community, individuals share stories of hope and resilience, inspiring others to find hope in their own journeys. By participating in hope-sharing discussions, accessing resilience-building resources, and celebrating milestones, members of The Safe Room community foster a culture of hope and support. Together, they demonstrate that even in the face of profound loss, hope can be nurtured, and new chapters of life can be written with renewed purpose and resilience.

Amidst the shadows of grief, Chapter 20 of "The Safe Room" unfolds as a poignant exploration into the transformative power of Cultivating Hope. In this chapter, we delve into the vital importance of nurturing hope during the grieving process, and within the supportive embrace of The Safe Room, we share stories that illuminate the resilient spirit's ability to blossom even in the midst of profound loss.

The Safe Room: A Garden of Hope:

Chapter 20 within The Safe Room paints a vivid picture of a garden where hope, resilient and blooming, becomes the heart of the grief journey. It celebrates the transformative power of hope, showcasing stories within the community that demonstrate the indomitable human spirit's ability to find light even in the shadows. As we cultivate hope together, within The Safe Room, the collective strength becomes a testament to the enduring nature of the human soul—a beacon of inspiration for those navigating grief's intricate paths.

CHAPTER 21

CONCLUSION

A Journey of Healing

In this final chapter, we recap key concepts and insights from the book and encourage readers to continue their healing journey within The Safe Room community and beyond.

Key Concepts and Insights Recap

1.1 Understanding Grief

Throughout this book, we explored the multifaceted nature of grief. We learned that grief is a natural response to loss and that it manifests differently for each individual. Grief can encompass a wide range of emotions, experiences, and challenges.

1.2 The Power of Connection and Support

We emphasized the importance of seeking and nurturing connections with others who understand the complexities of grief. The Safe Room community provides a safe and empathetic space where individuals can find support, share stories, and learn from one another.

1.3 Coping Strategies and Self-Care

We discussed various coping strategies, such as self-care practices, seeking professional help, and engaging in activities that promote healing and well-being. These strategies empower individuals to navigate grief and cultivate resilience.

1.4 Honoring and Remembering

We explored the significance of honoring and remembering loved ones. Rituals, traditions, and meaningful actions can help individuals find solace and keep the memories of their loved ones alive.

Section 2: Continuing the Healing Journey

2.1 The Safe Room as a Supportive Community

We encourage readers to continue their healing journey within The Safe Room community. The community offers a wealth of resources, support groups, discussions, and events tailored to the needs of those navigating grief. Engaging with the community can provide ongoing support and connection.

2.2 Embracing Growth and Resilience

We remind readers that healing is a nonlinear process. It involves ups and downs, setbacks and breakthroughs. It is important to embrace the growth and resilience that can emerge from the grief journey. The Safe Room community provides a platform to share stories of hope, resilience, and personal triumphs, inspiring others on their own paths.

2.3 Beyond The Safe Room

While The Safe Room community is a valuable resource, it is also essential to seek support and resources outside of the community. This may include connecting with local support groups, engaging in therapy or counseling, or exploring additional resources that align with individual needs and preferences.

2.4 The Continuing Journey

Grief is a lifelong journey, and healing takes time. It is crucial to be patient and compassionate with oneself. The Safe Room community and other resources can serve as a compass and guiding light on this ongoing journey.

Conclusion:

In this book, we have explored the complexities of grief and provided insights, coping strategies, and support resources within The Safe Room community. We have emphasized the importance of connection, self-care, and honoring loved ones. As you continue your healing journey, we encourage you to lean on the support available within The Safe Room, engage with the community, and embrace the growth and resilience that arise from your experiences. Remember, healing is a personal and unique process. May your journey be one of hope, connection, and transformation.

The Safe Room community organizes various events and discussions that readers should look out for. Here are a few examples:

1. Healing Circles: These are facilitated group discussions focused on specific aspects of grief and healing. Topics may include coping with anniversaries, navigating holidays, finding meaning in loss, or exploring self-care practices. Healing Circles provide a safe and supportive space for members to share their experiences, learn from one another, and gain valuable insights.

2. Guest Speaker Series: The Safe Room often invites guest speakers, including grief counselors, psychologists, authors, and individuals who have experienced profound loss and found resilience. These speakers share their expertise, personal stories, and strategies for healing. Attending these sessions can offer new perspectives and practical tools for the grief journey.

3. Virtual Workshops and Retreats: The Safe Room community occasionally hosts virtual workshops and retreats that delve deeper into specific aspects of grief and healing. These events provide opportunities for interactive learning, guided activities, and connection with other participants. Workshops and retreats cover topics such as creative expression, mindfulness practices, and building resilience.

4. Monthly Themes and Challenges: The Safe Room community often introduces monthly themes or challenges to engage members

in focused discussions and activities related to grief and healing. These themes can range from self-compassion and gratitude to exploring new hobbies or finding ways to honor loved ones. Participating in these monthly initiatives can foster personal growth and connection within the community.

5. Peer Support Groups: The Safe Room offers peer support groups that bring together individuals who share similar experiences or loss. These groups provide a dedicated space for members to connect, share their stories, and offer support to one another. Peer support groups promote a sense of belonging and understanding as members navigate their grief journeys together.

To stay updated on upcoming events and discussions within The Safe Room community, readers can access the community's online platform or subscribe to newsletters and notifications. Engaging with these events and discussions can further enrich the healing journey and provide a sense of community and support.

As we stand at the threshold of the concluding chapter in "The Safe Room," it is not merely an endpoint but a gateway to new beginnings—a beacon of hope illuminating the path forward. Chapter 21, "A Journey of Healing," invites you to reflect on the transformative insights woven throughout this book and encourages you to embrace the ongoing process of healing within The Safe Room and beyond.

Recap of Key Concepts:

1. The Sanctuary of The Safe Room:

- From the very beginning, we introduced The Safe Room as a sanctuary—a space transcending physical boundaries where empathy, understanding, and support converge to create a haven for those navigating grief.

2. SAFEROOM: A Mnemonic for Healing:

- SAFEROOM, the guiding mnemonic, encapsulates the foundational principles within The Safe Room: Support, Acknowledgment, Fellowship, Empathy, Resources, Openness, Opportunity, and Moderation. These principles form the bedrock of our shared journey.

3. Navigating the Landscape of Grief:

- Chapters unfolded as portals, guiding you through the diverse landscapes of grief. From sympathetic listening to cultivating hope, each chapter explored essential facets of the healing journey.

Encouragement for Continued Healing:

1. Community as a Healing Force:

- The Safe Room is not just a book; it is a living, breathing community of individuals who understand the intricate tapestry of grief. Continue to draw strength from the collective experiences, stories, and support found within The Safe Room.

2. Beyond These Pages:

- The journey does not end here. The Safe Room extends beyond these pages, inviting you to explore, share, and connect. Embrace the community as a source of ongoing solace, understanding, and companionship.

3. Your Unique Healing Path:

- Recognize that healing is a deeply personal journey. The insights shared within this book serve as signposts, but your path is uniquely yours. Embrace the ebb and flow of healing, allowing yourself the grace to navigate at your own pace.

Embracing Tomorrow's Light:

1. Continued Self-Exploration:

- The conclusion of this book marks the beginning of a new phase in your healing journey. Continue to explore the layers of your emotions, lean on the support of The Safe Room community, and foster a sense of resilience.

2. Celebrate Progress, No Matter How Small:

- Healing is not linear, and every small step forward is a victory. Celebrate your progress, honor your resilience, and acknowledge the courage it takes to confront and embrace the complexities of grief.

3. Fostering Hope:

- Cultivate hope as a constant companion. The stories shared within The Safe Room are testaments to the human spirit's ability to find light even in the darkest moments. Let hope be a guiding force as you navigate the twists and turns of your healing journey.

A Grateful Farewell:

As we bid farewell to the pages of "The Safe Room," know that you carry with you the collective wisdom, empathy, and support of a community that extends beyond these words. May this book be a cherished companion, offering comfort, guidance, and a reminder that you are not alone.

In your hands, you hold more than a book; you hold the potential for healing, growth, and a renewed sense of purpose. The journey continues, and within The Safe Room, the light of understanding and companionship will always guide your way.

Farewell, dear reader, and may your path be illuminated by the gentle glow of healing, resilience, and the enduring light of hope.

GLOSSARY

1. Grief: The intense emotional response to a loss, particularly the death of a loved one.

2. Bereavement: The state of having suffered a loss, especially through the death of a loved one.

3. Mourning: The process of expressing grief, often through rituals, ceremonies, or other cultural practices.

4. Loss: The experience of being deprived of someone or something significant.

5. Coping: The strategies and mechanisms individuals use to

manage and adapt to the challenges of grief.

6. Support: Assistance, encouragement, and comfort provided to someone who is grieving.

7. Grief counseling: Professional guidance and support provided by trained counselors to individuals experiencing grief.

8. Support group: A gathering of individuals who have experienced similar losses, providing mutual support and understanding.

9. Complicated grief: Prolonged or intense grief that interferes with daily functioning and requires specialized intervention.

10. Anticipatory grief: The grief experienced before an expected loss or death occurs, often associated with terminal illnesses or long-term caregiving.

11. Denial: A defense mechanism where individuals refuse to accept the reality of a loss, often as an initial response to grief.

12. Anger: A common emotional response in grief characterized by feelings of resentment, frustration, or rage.

13. Bargaining: A stage of grief where individuals may attempt to negotiate with a higher power or fate, seeking to reverse or alter the loss.

14. Depression: A deep and prolonged sadness that can accompany grief, often characterized by feelings of hopelessness, emptiness, and withdrawal.

15. Acceptance: The final stage of grief, where individuals come to terms with the loss and begin to adjust to a new reality.

16. Resilience: The ability to adapt and recover from adversity, including the challenges of grief.

17. Triggers: Events, objects, or situations that evoke strong emotional responses or memories associated with the loss.

18. Anniversary reaction: Heightened grief or emotional responses triggered by the anniversary of a significant loss.

19. Remembrance: The act of honoring and preserving memories of the deceased, often through rituals, memorials, or personal tributes.

20. Closure: A sense of resolution or completion regarding the loss, allowing individuals to move forward in the grieving process.

21. Compassion fatigue: Emotional exhaustion and reduced empathy experienced by individuals providing support to those who are grieving.

22. Empathy: The ability to understand and share the feelings of another person, often expressed through compassionate actions and listening.

23. Self-care: Practices and activities that promote physical, emotional, and mental well-being to maintain one's own health and resilience.

24. Rituals: Symbolic acts or ceremonies performed to honor, remember, or commemorate the deceased.

25. Death doulas: Trained professionals who provide emotional, practical, and spiritual support to individuals nearing the end of life and their families.

26. Eulogy: A speech or tribute given at a funeral or memorial service in honor of the deceased.

27. Hospice care: Specialized medical care and support provided to individuals with life-limiting illnesses, focusing on comfort, pain management, and quality of life.

28. Palliative care: Medical care aimed at managing symptoms and improving the quality of life for individuals with serious illnesses, including during the end-of-life stage.

29. Legacy: The impact, memories, and contributions left behind by an individual after their death.

30. Death positivity: A movement that encourages open conversations, acceptance, and understanding of death as a natural part of life.

31. Sympathy: Expressing condolences or feelings of sorrow for someone else's loss.

32. Empowerment: Supporting individuals in their grief journey by helping them regain a sense of control, choice, and strength.

33. Trauma: Emotional and psychological distress resulting from a distressing or disturbing event, such as a sudden or violent loss.

34. Post-traumatic stress disorder (PTSD): A mental health condition that can develop after experiencing or witnessing a traumatic event, often associated with symptoms like flashbacks, nightmares, and anxiety.

35. Closure ceremony: A gathering or ritual that provides a sense of closure and finality after a loss, often involving symbolic actions or releasing activities.

36. Respite care: Temporary relief and support provided to caregivers to alleviate stress and allow for rest and self-care.

37. Validation: Recognizing and acknowledging the emotions,

experiences, and reactions of someone who is grieving as valid and understandable.

38. Anniversary date: The specific date each year that marks the loss or death of a loved one.

39. Death anxiety: The fear or apprehension related to death, dying, or the unknown aspects of the afterlife.

40. Life review: A reflective process where individuals recall and evaluate their life experiences, often used as a therapeutic tool in grief counseling.

41. Transitional objects: Items or possessions that provide comfort and a sense of connection to the deceased, such as jewelry,photographs, or keepsakes.

42. Supportive listening: A communication technique that involves actively and empathetically listening to someone's thoughts, feelings, and experiences without judgment or interruption.

43. Coping mechanisms: Personal strategies and behaviors individuals use to manage stress, emotions, and grief.

44. Gratitude practice: A deliberate focus on expressing gratitude for the positive aspects of life, which can help cultivate a sense of hope and appreciation.

45. Self-reflection: The process of introspection and examining one's thoughts, feelings, and behaviors to gain insight and self-awareness.

46. Active coping: Engaging in proactive and constructive actions to address and manage the challenges of grief.

47. Trigger warning: A content advisory that alerts individuals to potentially distressing or triggering material, allowing them to make an informed decision about engaging with it.

48. Coping skills: Techniques, strategies, and practices that individuals develop to effectively manage and navigate grief.

49. Stages of grief: The commonly recognized patterns or phases that individuals may experience during the grieving process, such as the Kübler-Ross model (denial, anger, bargaining, depression, acceptance).

50. Hope: A positive and optimistic belief in the possibility of positive outcomes, growth, and healing, even in the face of loss and adversity.

REFERENCE

Downes, A. (2022). The Safe Place. St. Martin's Publishing Group.

- Didion, J. (2005). The Year of Magical Thinking. Alfred A. Knopf.

- Schwiebert, P., & DeKlyen, C. (1999). Tear Soup: A Recipe for Healing After Loss. Grief Watch.

- Sandberg, S., & Grant, A. (2017). Option B: Facing Adversity, Building Resilience, and Finding Joy. Ebury Publishing.

- James, J. W., & Friedman, R. (2009). The Grief Recovery Handbook: The Action Program for Moving Beyond Death, Divorce, and Other Losses. HarperCollins.

- Lewis, C. S. (1961). A Grief Observed. Faber and Faber.

- Kalanithi, P. (2016). When Breath Becomes Air. Random House.

- Hickman, M. W. (1994). Healing After Loss: Daily Meditations for Working Through Grief. HarperCollins.

- Young, K. (Ed.). (2010). The Art of Losing: Poems of Grief and Healing. Bloomsbury Publishing USA.

- Weller, F. (2015). The Wild Edge of Sorrow: Rituals of Renewal and the Sacred Work of Grief. North Atlantic Books.

ABOUT THE AUTHOR

Ekene Sabastine Aniakor is an expert disaster manager and grief and trauma counselor. He was born on July 3rd, 1982 in Onitsha, Anambra State, Nigeria. With a dedication, passion, and approachable demeanor, he brings exceptional problem-solving skills and a deep interest in grief management.

Ekene draws upon a rich vein of personal experiences in grief situations, having successfully navigated the challenges of his twelve-year marriage, which included the loss of a child at birth and the heartbreaking climax of losing his spouse, who was seven months pregnant with a set of twins. These experiences have shaped him into a compassionate and empathetic counselor, offering valuable insights and support to clients facing similar situations.

Having gained an excellent understanding of mental health issues through personal experiences and previous work with the Ministry of Passion of the Wound of our Lord Jesus Christ, Sabastine seeks to establish a grief counseling school in the United States. His ultimate goal is to create a safe space for clients outside of conventional institutions, providing them with the necessary tools to navigate the complexities of grief and trauma.

Currently serving as a Grief Manager at the Ministry of the Passion of the Wound of our Lord Jesus Christ, Sabastine has made significant contributions in his role. He developed and implemented counseling plans for Catholic men who lost loved ones in the tragic Owo church attack, offering support and solace during their time of grief. Additionally, he organized workshops and trainings for teachers, equipping them with the skills to counsel traumatized children.

Ekene holds a B.A. in English Education from Nasarawa State University, Keffi. Prior to this, he completed his secondary education at Amansiodo Boys Secondary School in Oghe, Enugu, Nigeria.

With his unwavering commitment to helping others and his wealth of experiences, Ekene Sabastine Aniakor is a beacon of hope and a guiding light for those navigating the turbulent seas of grief and trauma. This is his first book.

The Safe Room

The Safe Room

The Safe Room